Interludes With The Gods

CELESTIAL ARTS
Berkeley, California

Sondra Ray

Cover design by Ken Scott
Cover photo of Mt. Kailas by Hugh Swift
Text design and composition by Jeff Brandenburg, ImageComp

FIRST PRINTING 1992

Library of Congress Cataloging-in-Publication Data

Ray, Sondra.
    Interludes with the Gods / Sondra Ray.
        p.   cm.
    ISBN 0-89087-635-5
    1. Ray, Sondra. 2. New Age movement — Biography. 3. Gurus.
I. Title.
BP605.N48R39 1991
299'.93 — dc20
[B]   91-18569
                                                                        CIP

1   2   3   4   5   /   95   94   93   92   91

Contents

I offer light to the holy supreme guru Lord of Mercy
Abode of truth consciousness and eternal bliss
Thou art without all but always residing in the heart
Thy image is full of compassion and so beautiful

Repetition of Thy name dries up the ocean of the world's misery
May there be only pure devotion at Thy holy feet
My only desire is to be attached to Thy form

Thy form is of extreme beauty and gentleness
Beyond form and formless at the same time
Filling the mind with bliss on seeing it
Gods, men and sages all say Hail Hail to Haidakhandi

We take shelter and surrender before the omnipotent Lord
Holy, peaceful, non-dual, remover of sins
The trinity remover of pain, doer of goodness

The guru is Brahma, the guru is Vishnu, the guru is Lord Shiva
The guru is verily the absolute one
That is why I bow to the holy guru

The image of the guru is the root of meditation
The feet of the guru are the root of worship
The speech of the guru is the root of mantras
The grace of the guru is the root of liberation

Endless like the shape of the circle
Encompassing the whole dynamic and static universe
To him who shows that abode of God to us
To that guru I bow

O Lord sitting in the siddha pose residing in solitude
Thou ocean of knowledge full of bliss
Of peaceful nature, pure and generous
Who frees us from bondage
Hail Hail O king of sages, remover of the pain of Thy devotees

Thy form is white and beautiful
Thy smiling holy face is lotus-like
Thy broad forehead has a third eye with very brilliant light
Thy big eyes overflow with the tears of love
Hail Hail O king of sages, remover of the pain of Thy devotees

In the darkness of illusion I do not see Thy form
In times of calamity I do not remember Thy name
Nor have I ever worshipped Thy holy feet which remove illusion
Hail Hail O king of sages, remover of the pain of Thy devotees

Thy greatness which is endless like the sky is told on Earth
The fame of Thy grandeur and sweetness reverberates everywhere
O Lord who liberates, have mercy on us!
Hail Hail O king of sages, remover of the pain of Thy devotees

Almighty Lord, the sustainer of the universe
I am dependent upon you alone
Thou who givest intellect to thy feeble-minded devotees
Destroyer of obstacles, destroy all hinderances
Hail Hail O king of sages, remover of the pain of Thy devotees

Whenever there is a decline of righteousness is the world
Then Thou comest in the world to save it
O destroyer of sins, cleanse us of all our defects
Hail Hail O king of sages, remover of the pain of Thy devotees

I surrender to Thee, O Lord, Thou alone are my refuge
Thou alone are my mother, my father, my kin, my all
Thou are my Lord in the world and the scriptures
Hail Hail O king of sages, remover of the pain of Thy devotees

Thine eyes are wet with compassion and full of mercy
O Lord let the whole creation be fulfilled by your merciful compassionate look
God's play, which Thou performest in human form put on, is wonderful
Hail Hail O king of sages, remover of the pain of Thy devotees

OM
Thou alone are mother and father to me
Thou alone are kin and friend to me
Thou alone are knowledge and wealth to me
Thou are all to me, my Lord, O Lord

Residing peacefully on beautiful Mount Kailash
Is that sage whose form always reflects compassion
To Him I constantly bow

By whose mere rememberance a devotee gains enlightenment
To Him the ultimate guru residing in Haidakhan I bow
By whose merciful look people become liberated
To His holy feet I bow continuously

I bow to Him whose heart is soft, whose speech is soft
Even whose stick is soft, whose body is soft
Thy vision is full of mercy

Thou who seest the moving and nonmoving universe
Who is always busy doing good in the world
To Thou, to whom attachment and jealousy are forbidden, I bow

Supreme guru, the foundation of all good qualities
Whose true meaning is hard to reach even through mediation
Truth, eternity, consciousness and bliss
I remember Him always

Thou are God (Vishnu) Himself as well as a devotee of God
Constantly doing meditation on God
By drinking the nectar of God's name
One attains God's holy eternal abode

Thou givest to the ignorant
True knowledge very difficult to attain
I am without any spiritual practice
Thou art my only refuge

Thou art great like the sun
Dispelling the darkness of illusion
The soul of all beings
Thou are the very life of Mahendra

Preface

In the course of learning what I now teach, I have been strongly influenced by each of the people described in this book. Some of them, such as my guru Babaji and Jesus, continue to guide me at all times.

Others I still learn from occasionally, and some have since taken paths that go in different directions than mine. I thank them all for the things they have taught me.

I thank all my enlightened teachers, especially those in this book. I thank them for their knowledge, awareness, love, guidance and spiritual generosity. I dedicate this book to them and honor them.

I bow to my supreme guru Hherakan Babaji, who is present everywhere. I thank him for my liberation and my joy. I thank him for blessing us with the great ones: Muniraj and Shastriji (who he described as two of the purest men on earth). Although there are no chapters specifically on them in this book, I have written about them in my book *Pure Joy*.

May everything I write be something beautiful for God.

— *Sondra Ray*

Leonard Orr

Founder of Rebirthing

❧

Leonard gave me the gift of rebirthing which totally healed me. He got me clear on creative thought, which is the secret to everything. He reminded me of physical immortality, which released me from death. He cleared me on the five biggies, which changed my life forever. He taught me how to be relaxed and how to let go of rigidity and too much form. He taught me how to lead seminars. He gave me my new career and reminded me of my life's purpose. He helped me to work through my father's death. He taught me about money and success. He led me to India and to my true guru, Babaji. He definitely gave me something to write about.

Before I met Leonard, I was living in Arizona, working as a nurse. I was searching for miracles, and I was not finding them in medicine, my own field. My hair was falling out . . . I was literally going bald. Besides that, I had a severe pain which I had had for years, since my father's death, to be exact. I had been wearing wigs for two years and feeling "desperate." It had been nearly two years since my divorce, and I had not recovered very well at all. Then my husband called, saying he wanted me back. "Maybe that is the answer," I thought. So I shipped all my things to Florida, where he was, and I was literally leaving the next day. However, that night I had my first real "mystical" experience. I was sitting on the floor talking to a friend of mine who was a dentist. I was talking about going back to my ex. Suddenly, I heard a voice outside my head actually, and I was filled with light. I could not move. The voice said, "*Never go back.*" I was stunned. Then it said it louder, "*Never go back. Go to California, now!*" I could not move. I was speechless. My friend said, "Sondra, I think you better go to California."

I knew no one in California, and in fact I had just received a letter from the California Nurses' Association, telling me that it did not matter if I had a Master's degree, there were no jobs available for nurses in California, so I should not come.

But, with that mystical experience, I would have been crazy not to go. The next morning I turned my Fiat toward California, even though my things were going the other direction! I went on sheer faith and guidance. I do not remember the trip at all. I went toward San Francisco because I had read about two researchers there who had appeared on the cover of *Time* magazine and I was interested in their work. Or at least that is why I *thought* I was going to San Francisco. My name was Sondra Scott at the time. My car literally *quit* on Scott Street in the Marina district. I looked up and saw a sign: "Furnished Apartment for Rent." (I definitely needed a furnished apartment!) I had no money, however. I had just blown it all, as usual, in Europe. I went up to the manager's office and said, "I need to live here."

He said, "Ma'am, you need first month's rent and last month's rent."

I said, "I know, but I need to live here."

He said, "Ma'am, you need first month's rent and last month's rent *plus* deposit for breakage."

"I know," I said. "But I need to live here."

We went back and forth. Finally, he looked at me and said, "I don't know what it is about you . . . I have never done this in twenty-five years . . . but I will let you move in."

From then on I had one miracle after another. I looked up the researchers I had read about. They had no funds for apprentices but they made a few calls and helped me get a job. Within one day I was hired at Kaiser Hospital in the prenatal clinic. It was perfect preparation for my career as a rebirther.

My local hairdresser introduced me to a client who became my first California friend, Karen. Karen led me to EST. After EST, everything opened up. However, I began to have a new problem: I started having car accidents. I began to get "rear-ended" a lot after the EST training. It got to the point my car would get rear-ended even when I was not in it. I would come out of a boutique and there it would be banged up. After about the eighth time, I was devastated. Now I had three serious problems. My hair was still falling out. I still had the pain, and now my car was getting banged up. I, at least, had somewhere to go — my EST graduate seminar. I ended up there one night crying. Two male EST graduates took me under their wing and asked me what was the matter. I told them about my car, etc. They said, "Don't worry, we will take you to Leonard Orr."

I said, "Who on earth is Leonard Orr?"

"Oh, he is a new guru in town . . . he was once Werner's consultant."

I was willing to try anything and anyone by this time.

So, Sunday morning they picked me up and drove me out to the woods. There was this man named Leonard with about 30 people sitting at his feet. He was drawing a bunch of dots on a flip chart. Then he talked about the "Five Biggies" (The Birth Trauma, the Parental Disapproval Syndrome, the Unconscious Death Urge, Specific Negatives and Other Lifetimes). I immediately knew this was it. I knew that somewhere in there was the cause of my big problems. I surrendered to him right off the bat. At the break, I went to him begging him to give me a private consultation. "You will have to come to my room at midnight," he said . . . which I thought was very strange. But, that was the only time he had, he claimed. So I did.

I wrote down all my problems on a piece of paper. I turned it in to him. I though that might save his time. He read them over carefully and asked which one I wanted to work on first. "The car," I said. "I cannot afford to drive anymore at the rate I am going with these accidents. I have to get to work . . ."

"Oh," he said, "This is easy."

"Easy?" I couldn't believe it was easy.

"Just write down, 'I now have a safe driving consciousness.' Write this affirmation ten times daily."

"That is it?" I couldn't believe that would do it.

Then he reminded me thoughts create results and affirmations would change results.

"Do you mean to say I could create men calling me on the phone using affirmation?" I wanted to know (there were some men I wanted to hear from).

"Oh, yes," he said.

"Well, what is the affirmation for that?" I begged.

"I now receive an abundance of phone calls from men," he replied.

So I went home and tested him. Of course I tried the affirmation about phone calls first. It worked! Like magic! All the men I wanted to hear from called me. Pretty soon, however, I started getting calls from men at night . . . wrong numbers, etc.

I though Mr. Orr had put a hex on me. I called him. "Leonard you have to reverse this thing . . . I can't sleep."

"Oh, just correct the affirmation" he said. "It is simple. Just write 'I now receive phone calls from only the men I want to hear from.'" It worked also. I wrote some about my car then. Even that worked.

I started following Leonard around, trying to figure out his magic.

One day I was sitting in an astrology class. Leonard walked in, saying from the back of the room, "Who wants to try this new thing I am doing called rebirthing?" My hand was up in the air and I could not get it down. *What had I volunteered for?*

Then he said we would have to drop out for five days and go away with him. Even though I was a nurse, I arranged it. It seemed impossible, but I did it.

And so Leonard took ten of us out in the woods in the Santa Cruz Mountains to a place that had been a nudist camp. The main feature for us was the hot tub. He was going to put us in there one at a time with a snorkel and try to rebirth us. We were scared. We were guinea pigs. He spent a long time sitting by the fire with us explaining it. He had discovered rebirthing by accident once when he went in the sauna and stayed in longer than the recommended time. They had found him on the floor, regressed to infancy, babbling like a baby. Later, when they pulled him out and he "came to," he was amazed he could remember his infancy like that. He was fascinated. About the same time he noticed that he was taking very long baths ... staying in the water for hours and hours and not wanting to get out. In fact, he felt like getting *under* the water and staying there. One day, during one of these long baths, he had a "spontaneous birth memory." This surprised him greatly because he did not know you could remember your birth. It also scared him because at his own birth, the umbilical cord was wrapped around his neck several times and he nearly died.

Gradually, he allowed himself to have these rebirth memories come out. He did this by continuing the long baths. He did this over a five-year period without discussing it with anyone until he was certain he knew what he was doing. And this is something I greatly appreciate about him. He continued until he broke through. One day he had a very mystical experience walking down the street. Everything became orgasmic, colorful, different. He knew he had discovered something.

Shortly after that he moved to San Francisco and became eager to try this on someone else. They got the idea of going in a hot tub with a snorkel. That person immediately had a birth memory. Wet rebirthing was born! So here we were, ten of us, willing to try it. Leonard had us get in sleeping bags and stay in them that night and very late the next morning. He made us stay in extra long to build up that "claustrophobia feeling" one gets when one wants to get out of the womb ("no exit terror"). It worked. We were all "psyched," "wired to the max," jumpy like a bunch of babies wanting to get born. He took us all down to the tub and rebirthed us one by one for the next two days. It was, for me, the single most important event in my life at that time. After I rebirthed I felt like a new person. After two rebirths I was hooked. After three rebirths, my pain went away and never came back. It was obviously the miracle I was looking for. Even my hair stopped falling out.

We all moved into an old house in the Haight Ashbury district and put a hot tub in the basement. Even before we had furniture, we had a hot tub. I was still working as a nurse, but one day I went up to Leonard and asked, "How do I become a rebirther?"

"Handle your own birth trauma" was his reply.

And so it began . . . living in the basement, hours, days, nights, weeks, and months we rebirthed each other and our friends. We all began to have miracles, and we couldn't stop talking about them. People would gather around me at parties in San Francisco. Sometimes I would be amazed to look up and find twenty or more people at a party gathered around me. That was easy for me. After all, I was passionately in love with the process. It had given me everything I had hoped for.

Soon, it became unethical for me to stay in nursing. Here I was passing out pills, having no guarantee whatsoever that patients would not get their illnesses back after going off the pills (many or most did), and what we were seeing at home with rebirthing was people getting healed permanently by just changing their thoughts and breathing. One day I put down my pills and I knew that chapter of my life was over. I threw myself into rebirthing completely. I studied spiritual healing. I turned over my whole life and my whole being to this work.

All of it wasn't easy. We were pioneers. Rebirthing was unheard of. Fortunately, California was tolerant. We were, even so, highly unusual. Our parents had trouble understanding how we could suddenly give up brilliant careers. Others wondered what we were doing working in the nude. The medical profession tried to tune us out altogether. What we went through the first two years as pioneers was so dramatic that I wrote a whole book on it, *Rebirthing in the New Age*. When people get rebirthed now, it seems like it is so simple that there is nothing to it. They have no idea how much we had to go through to take it to the place it is now. We did not even discover dry rebirthing for the first couple of years. That changed everything. I am very grateful that I stuck it out and that I had the privilege of having two straight years of wet rebirthing, even though it was so intense that way. It is one of the reasons I am where I am today.

And so Leonard began traveling. I ran Theta House when he was away. One day he came home and said, "They want you in Hawaii to come and speak. I told them you were coming . . ."

"What?" I started to protest . . . but that was Leonard.

Suddenly, I was on the road . . . a seminar leader. It happened overnight.

Living with Leonard was one of the wildest, most unusual experiences of my life. I was a good student. I began seriously researching the effects of birth trauma on relationships. The information was so exciting that it rapidly became obvious that should be my life's work. My mission became clear to me: world peace through the understanding of harmonious relationships and relationship technology. I thank Leonard for getting me back on purpose. The Loving Relationships Training, which I founded, grew out of this research. Rebirthing is at the very core of it.

I must also acknowledge Leonard for being one of the first immortalists to have the guts to speak out publicly on the subject in America. Back when he started doing that, the idea was not very acceptable at all. I was his chauffeur then, and I was with him a lot. We would be doing something simple like buying a pair of shoes; and there he would be teaching the shoe salesman about immortality! I would be embarrassed but I secretly admired his guts. I decided that if he could be that brave, so could I. I would stick my neck out and write a book containing these ideas . . . as a way of serving the community and as my way of acknowledging Leonard.

I remember one night we sat in the dining room and tossed the *I Ching*. We asked the *I Ching* if it was time to put out the concept of physical immortality in writing. The *I Ching* said, "Yes, but you are on very thin ice."

I went through a lot writing that. It all came to a head when we were in Walton, New York, Leonard's home town. I was trying to finish that chapter (I tell this story here in closing as acknowledgement to Leonard). While typing, my joints suddenly became stiff and painful. I seemed to be having an attack of early arthritis. Of course, I knew the symptoms from nursing. I was horrified. I also could not believe it was happening to me. Nobody in my family had arthritis! Why me? My writing career was just beginning. Was I now suddenly ruined forever? I went crazy. I ran to Leonard's room crying . . . and shouting, "*Leonard, I have arthritis!*"

His answer was stunning.

"Oh, this is great," he said. "Now I never have to worry about you again."

"What?" I cried, "I don't get it."

"Oh, you are just going through your old age early . . . this is good," he insisted.

"Oh," I said, immediately feeling better.

I went out of there happy. I knew it would go away. It took me two weeks to process out arthritis. I was also crippled, senile, and couldn't hear. Only an immortalist could have cleared me on that. Old age was hard. I did not like it. But I learned it was just programming and I could "process it out."

Then I became younger. Some days I would look nine years old.

Other days I would look ninety.

For the next year my age would change continually.

I had one more attack of old age that year after a Rolfing session. Leonard put me to bed and told me to sink into it. He would bring me juice. Another time I became a baby. Leonard had me crawl around the floor in front of everyone at the seminar . . . just like a toddler. Then he told people to hold me and feed me with a bottle.

After this, I gave up age. I became eternal.

I "graduated."

And then he took me to India. That was a real miracle. Finding Babaji. That is when our real work began . . .

Over the years we have both changed a lot. Today I feel complete with Leonard. I send him love.

Morna Simeona

Kahuna

❧

I had always wanted to meet a real live Kahuna. I had heard of their healing powers and their control over the elements. I was living in Hawaii for a time and had the privilege of having Dr. Bill and Sue Hindle attend my LRT seminar one weekend. Later they threw a little luncheon party for me, my boyfriend Gary, and my organizer, Roger Lane. I had waited so long for this! I knew she was going to be my first "female guru," but I had no idea what to expect. When she walked in, I burst into tears. She was so beautiful. Her presence was so wonderful, so immense! She seemed like a full woman and man at the same time. I melted down very fast. I recovered just enough to be seated at the table next to her for lunch. I was so thrilled. Suddenly, to my surprise, I was totally "prostrated" with my head actually in my plate sobbing. I heard her saying, "Peace be with you . . ." I finally looked up at her, half bowing over my plate and I managed to ask her if she would mind telling me what she was doing!

"Oh, just a little crystal cleansing," she quipped. My boyfriend suddenly had his head in his plate at the other end of the table. He was sobbing also. Our friend Roger suddenly disappeared also and had to go lie down . . . found him crying on the bed. We all got through that and proceeded, almost as if nothing had happened. Then Sue Hindle, the hostess, was waiting for the food. When it did not come she called out to Paul (the LRT graduate she had hired as the chef to cater the luncheon). He was supposed to be serving us the quiche. However, we found him on the floor sobbing.

So that was my first experience of Morna.

Several months later, I decided I needed her to do an "exorcism" on the beach house Gary and I were living in. Gary could never sleep . . . he kept seeing spears flying. (There *was* something unusual going on in this beautiful home.) I went to Morna and she agreed to come out. I drove her out in my sports car with the top down. It was really something. Half way out to Waimanelo she raised her voice: "What is going on in the southeast corner of your house?" she demanded.

"I don't know Morna . . ."

When we got to the house, she went immediately to the swimming pool as if she knew exactly where to go. She had a "fit." "This rock should have never been removed from the big island," she protested, when she saw the big lava rock at the bottom of the pool. "The Gods are angry," she insisted.

"What do we do?" I asked.

"Well," she said, "I will try to transmute it, but I can't guarantee anything. Also, this house was built over an old Hawaiian fish hatchery, which should have never happened."

Somehow I knew the house was "doomed."

I left her alone. Once during the next hour, I peered over the balcony looking at her sitting by the pool. I swear she had transfigured. She looked just like a man . . .

Later we moved at her recommendation.

Once I went to visit Morna for a consultation. I asked her what she was thinking about that day. "Oh," she said, "I am studying the ocean floor around Russia."

Another time I went to see her early in the morning. She had been up since 3 A.M. praying for three thousand souls, she said. That day she told me that Hawaii would always be my second home. She also said it was a miracle that I had gotten out of a certain Hawaii cave alive. (I had shared with her an apparition I had in a cave in Maui.)

Another time I went to her for reassurance when there was so much talk about the 1984 "prophesies of doom." People were nervous. There was a lot of talk about California falling into the ocean. I asked her about this. She replied that that would never happen because the waves would affect the Hawaiian Islands. She looked right at me and said, "You don't really think I would let anything happen to the Hawaiian Islands do you? Besides, Sondra, I am taking care of it. I am draining the energy all off Kahoolawe." (A deserted island used as a bombing range.) She put me right at ease.

Another time I went to visit her with manuscript in hand. The manuscript was *Celebration of Breath*. I had written it in Hawaii. I asked her to bless it. She held it in her lap for twenty minutes exactly, "charging it up." When the book came out, I noticed people "grabbed it." They couldn't seem to wait to get their hands on it.

Before my 1984 world tour, I received an instruction to go to Hawaii and be with my teachers. I got an appointment with Morna at high noon, Easter Sunday, 1984. She was not into saying much. She merely did the Ho'O'ponopono process on me, clearing all my ancestors and karmic ties. She had me fill out papers and then tear them up and then say Hawaiian prayers. She seemed to "absorb my karma" or something that day. I had the feeling she was also initiating me into the world ministry. She said very little to me that day. It was not necessary. Something else was happening.

A few hours later, I was in a very deep spontaneous rebirth, breathing like mad in my hotel room. Morna's presence was everywhere; like purple light, it roared through with such a force I was nearly knocked over. I remember shouting out "Okay, Morna, let's run with this!"

Still, today, I honor the process of Ho'O'ponopono, though I have not seen Morna for many years.

Ida Rolf

Founder of Rolfing

🜚

I had about twelve Rolfing sessions and had received tremendous value from Rolfing. My whole body had changed. I really wanted to meet this woman, Ida Rolf. I knew she had to be something very special. One day Leonard invited her over to the house to try rebirthing. I got elected to rebirth her. She was already in her eighties, walking with a cane. She came in, and I was in love with her on the spot. She obviously liked me, too. She pointed her cane at parts of my body, saying "not deep enough" . . . meaning the Rolfing I had had; and she wanted to know who my Rolfer had been. We went down to the basement and I put her in the tub. She was very hesitant to put her head under water. She kept stopping the rebirthing and telling me how I should Rolf her body this way and that. I kept saying, "Hey Ida, I am supposed to be rebirthing you, not Rolfing you." She was amazing. She kept testing me. I finally got her to put her head under the water. Afterwards, she got out of the tub and decided to walk without her cane. She also told Leonard that the rebirthing had improved her eyesight. Then she called us both into the living room by the fireplace for a private chat. She sat us both down and looked us in the eyes . . .

"Now," she said, "I have something to tell you. I figured out physical immortality all by myself when I was age thirty-three. But I couldn't hang on to the concept because there was no agreement. I was already thrown out of the universities for being too radical, too ahead of my time. I couldn't talk to anyone about it. I finally gave up. But *don't you two ever give up!*"

With that she left.

I adored her.

I had a lot more Rolfings over the years. I think I had about a hundred and sixty when I stopped counting. I still like it, and I am convinced Rolfers are New Age sculptors. Ida was a genius.

I saw Ida the last time at the first Burklyn Business School. She was the guest of honor along with Bucky Fuller during the last week. She was going blind. I told her that I used to read to the blind in college so she asked me to read to her. I read to her from the *Autobiography of Yogi*. She was always able to pronounce difficult words I stumbled over. She seemed also to be on a line ahead or two of where I was. Obviously she had some other kinds of visual powers that I didn't understand.

The last thing she ever said to me was: "Sondra, put that book down. Read to me from your own books."

Shortly after that I was teaching a seminar in Boulder, Colorado. It was held at the Rolfing Institute. Her picture was on the wall in front of me. She seemed to be looking down at me the whole time, blessing me with so much love. I was so filled with gratitude after that seminar that I went to my room and wrote her a very long letter promising her to carry on her work forever by telling people about it in all of my seminars. I found out she got that letter right before she died.

Sometimes when gifted Rolfers work on me, they say she is there. Once I saw her hovering nearby.

Ram Dass

The first time I met Ram Dass, he was giving a speech in Marin County. He came into my life at the perfect time, saying the perfect thing. I was leaving for India the next day, and I really needed to hear what he had to say.

He was telling stories about his guru's guru. Once there was this devotee, he said, who did every single thing the guru said. She could not think for herself. She had no mind of her own. And so, the guru decided to clear her on this. One day he told her to go out and buy an ice cream cone. And then he told her to buy some mustard also. And then he told her to come back to him with the ice cream cone in hand and the mustard, and sit at his feet, and so she did. And then he told her to put the mustard on the ice cream cone and eat it. And she did. And then he threw her out for being so stupid.

I vowed that I would never forget that story.

I vowed that I would have self esteem and think for myself, even in the presence of the guru. After all, I did not want to be thrown out!

The next day I left for my first trip to Babaji.

He tested me constantly on my self esteem. I never forgot the story. I told him my feelings, my thoughts. I was *me* in his presence. He respected me.

I will always be grateful to Ram Dass for sharing that story. Somehow my getting to his lectures has always been at the right time. The last time I heard from him, he prepared me for the nineties.

Swami Satchitananda

I was walking down the street one day in Santa Barbara with my friend, Bobby Birdsall. We passed a toy store. "We have to go in here," he said. "Why," I wanted to know . . . I really didn't want to buy any toys right then. "Do you want a toy?" I asked.

"No," Bobby said, "But for some reason we need to go in here." In he went.

Inside the store, I could not believe my eyes. I started to cry. I saw the most beautiful Saint in there buying toys! He was wearing soft orange silk robes. He was gorgeous . . . glowing . . . absolute sweetness. I thought I was seeing things, but he was real. It was my first glimpse of Swami Satchitananda. He had a Yoga School in Santa Barbara. Bobby asked him if he wanted to go roller skating! I could never forget his beauty, his sweetness.

A year later I was meeting a man at the airport in Los Angeles. I was suddenly "blinded" by white light. There was Swami Satchitananda getting off the plane in front of my friend. I started to cry again. He remembered me.

Once I went to a talk he was giving. I was late. There was still music playing on the stage when I finally arrived, and I was so relieved that I had not missed any of his talk. I was running to a seat and I ran right into the Swami in the hall. There we

19

were again. There I was again, crying. He always has that effect on me.

Recently, I took our entire class of global warriors to hear him speak in Hawaii. He talked about world peace.

He keeps reminding me to become neutral, zero . . .

He can.

Swami Muktananda

❧

I was only able to see him twice before he left. He had a large
tent in Santa Monica. There were hundreds of people sitting
in lotus positions. Men on one side, women on the other. The
lights were turned down, and people began chanting. I did not
really understand chanting then. The lights went back on, and
there he was. How fabulous he was! I went up for *darshan* and
he tapped me with the peacock feather. I thank him for getting
me used to chanting.

A few years later, after I had been to India and had begun to
surrender to chanting, I thought of him again. I was beginning
to meet many of his devotees, and I liked them very much. I
wanted to return to India and take a friend with me to Babaji.
I said to this person, "You will have to get used to chanting."
He grumbled and grumbled. I told him that if he did not
change his attitude about chanting, it would not work, because
we often chanted for four to five hours a day in the temple. He
continued to grumble. I did not think he should go. But then,
that night, I found out Swami Muktananda was back in town.
I took my friend to the big tent. There was chanting for hours.
When we came home from the tent, my friend began to vomit.
He vomited and vomited and vomited. Afterwards I said,

"Okay, you can go with me now. Swami Muktananda has cured you of your resistance to chanting."

Later I was so grateful to the Swami for that, because it was very important that this friend went with me to India.

And I acknowledge Swami for his wonderful choice of a successor Guru Mai, or Swami Chidvalasananda. She is simply marvelous.

Abubabaji in India

My First Indian Teacher in India

🜋

We had been working with rebirthing less than two years when Leonard one day got a letter from India. It was a strange letter. It was addressed in pencil in a child's printing. There was no return address and the postscript was blurred. The city where it was from could not be made out. One could barely make out the country: India. Neither Leonard nor I knew anyone in India. Inside was some yellow "school paper" which looked as old as a country school would have had. Again the letter was printed in pencil in a child's handwriting. It was not signed. All it said was this: "*Come to India.*"

That was it. I remember saying something like, "Leonard we better go." I immediately knew he would go, and I wanted to go with him, though it was out of the question for me. I had just given up my high paying nursing job to learn to be a rebirther. I had just blown all my savings on a trip to Europe. I had no money at all. In a very short time Leonard was holding a "planning meeting" in the dining room of Theta House. I could not stay out of the room. I decided I had to go, no matter what. I had never ever borrowed money before, nor even tried to ask for any from anyone. The very idea just terrified me. However, I went to the phone and called Dr. Hindle and his wife in Hawaii who had been in one of my seminars. I told them I needed to go to India for my spiritual enlightenment. They said, "Pick up the money tomorrow . . . we will wire it to Beverly Hills." I couldn't get over it. I will always acknowledge Dr. Bill and Sue Hindle for that experience.

Leonard took about ten of us along. We landed in Bombay. It was as good as any city to start out with since we had no idea where we were going and who we were looking for. Diane had decided to go off alone. She went north. I went south with my boyfriend to see Rajneesh. Leonard walked around Bombay, stumbling on a high Yogi, named Abubabaji. At first we thought maybe he was our guru. He turned out to be our "preparation" for which we were later grateful. I had agreed to meet Leonard in a few days upon return. When we returned, we found him sitting at the feet of Abubabaji. I remember staying up most of the night listening to his stories. He told us how he had been raised in one of the wealthiest families of India. One could feel that. And how he was asked to give it all up and "start walking" and keep walking until further notice. An angel appeared to him. We were spellbound when he told us how he had walked for twenty some years, his clothes having fallen off after the first seven years. He told us how he had mastered the cold and the heat. One story I remember so well was when he was in the jungle and had not found food and was exhausted. He fell to the ground and started to die. A mother deer feeding her fawn came over and stuck her full tit in his mouth and fed him milk. Another time he was freezing in the Himalayas. He did not have any clothes and he was freezing to death. He looked up and saw a big avalanche coming down at him. He knew it was the end. Suddenly he realized it was really two huge polar bears instead, rushing down at him. He knew he had had it. He laid down and gave up. They came to a screeching halt and one sat on each side of him. Then they proceeded to calmly place their bodies over him to keep him warm. They came every night like that and kept him warm.

He had many stories like that. He also told us once he went for years without eating. I believed these stories. One just could tell they were true. Besides, we had read the *Life and Teachings of the Masters of the Far East*, and we had been mentally prepared to find Saints like this. We knew they existed. We had hoped to find one. Then he told us how after years of this rigorous training in the wilderness he was told to stop walking and come back to civilization and start healing. And his healing powers were very great! He was known around India for being able to heal poisonous lethal snake bites by long distance. We became fascinated with him.

He taught us about chanting and Indian ways. We finally invited him to the U.S. That is when he really "put us through it." We had what we thought was a great tour scheduled for him. He would however, change it every single day. This became a big problem since we had arranged for groups to see him in many cities. He changed the schedule at whim so many times that we "gave up." I remember Leonard finally throwing it up in the air. Abubabaji trained us to let go of control and the Western mind. I only came to really appreciate that nine years later.

I remember at the end of that U.S. tour Leonard and I had planned to take him to Disneyland. When I told him he looked at me with a twinkle in his eye and replied "*Disneyland!?* Sondra, I am *always* in Disneyland!" Yes, well that was that. I got that he was.

He returned to India.

Meanwhile, Diane returned with the news she had found Babaji, Hherakan Baba, the guru who was the hero of the book *Autobiography of a Yogi.* That was it! We decided to go back to India as soon as possible! On the way we stopped in New Delhi for Abubabaji's birthday. It was a celebration in a huge tent. Thousands were there. It was the one time he allowed himself to receive. The rest of the year he gave and gave. I had spent months before preparing his gift. I had written a poem and had it all done up in gold calligraphy on a scroll, beautifully framed.

I remember waiting two hours in line just to lay it at his feet. When I did, so much love welled up in me because of the receptive state he was in, that I had an orgasmic like experience I shall never forget. He really taught me how it heals people to let them give to you. I was healed because he let me give to him. It was a glorious day. But something happened that day. Leonard and he got in a major confrontation. I remember him yelling at Leonard. I remember Leonard turning completely green.

Leonard then came over to me, saying, "Come on Sondra, let's go. I am going to find the real Babaji up north Diane told us about. *You come with me.*"

But then Abubabaji came up to me and said "No, Sondra Ray, *you stay with me.*"

I was completely torn apart. Here I had my American guru pulling me one direction and my Indian guru pulling me another direction. They seemed equally powerful. I became paralyzed. I couldn't move.

Leonard left me alone.

An hour later I was still paralyzed — terrified to make the wrong decision.

Leonard came back saying: "Look, I decided to go alone anyway. You get your head together and meet me in three days. Go to Haldwani and ask for Muniraj."

And he was gone!

There I was, alone, paralyzed. For three days I could barely move. I was like glue. Everything was like glue. I could not think nor make any decisions. (See page 44 for the outcome of this.)

Saibaba in India

❊

"The most beneficial thing that can happen to a person is that he should draw God's love to himself," Saibaba once said.

I remember exactly the first time I drew Saibaba's love to me. It was in Paris, just after my very first trip to India. We had stopped to see some wealthy French people we had met the year before in the States. They lived in a penthouse near the Eiffel Tower. They had become Saibaba devotees that year and decided to show us home movies of Saibaba at his ashram. The film had barely started rolling when there was a sudden blackout. During the blackout, our host claimed that he had received a "message" from Saibaba to give us a "treat" of *Amrit*. Neither my boyfriend or I had any idea what that was. The host went to fetch a tiny precious urn. Inside was a special nectar . . . a nectar which had been materialized out of the body of Saibaba! I had read and heard about Saibaba's ability to materialize *vibuti* (sacred ash), so I had no trouble accepting this; however, I had not heard of the nectar, so I was very, very intrigued. When he poured a few drops of the precious nectar in the palm of my hand, I was very overcome. When I tasted it, I was truly humbled, and I remember saying to myself: "Sondra, this is probably a once-in-a-lifetime experience." It was truly the most divine taste imaginable.

Years later in Seattle, Washington I was going out with a man I consider to be one of the world's leading wine tasting experts. One night around 11:30 P.M. I was feeling a desire to give him something. I said to him: "Robert, the greatest gift I could give you right now would be this sacred elixir materialized out of Saibaba's body. It is the most divine taste possible." He, of course, loved the idea! "But," I said, "we have to go to Paris where I can perhaps get a drop or two, or to India."

In that very second, a miracle happened. A Saibaba devotee, Michelle, who had been one of my students, walked in the door. She had just returned from India, and she said, "Do you want some?" I nearly keeled over. First of all, I did not know she had been back to India. And second of all, how did she happen to be walking in the door at that very moment at that very house where we were?

"Are your serious?" I called out.

"Yes," she said, "I just happen to have a little. I sat under a shrine for six hours, collecting drops . . . it was dripping out of his picture." With *that* she left to fetch it. I woke up everyone in the house where I was staying. I told everyone to wash their hands and start meditating. Then we chanted. In no time at all, Michelle returned with a plastic bottle from India. She poured a little nectar in my hand. It looked unmistakedly the same. It tasted the same. I was thrilled. Everyone was thrilled. And then I looked again and the amount had *increased* in my palm! It seemed *alive*! My mind could not register that, however. I said, "This can't be happening." (Of course then it immediately stopped increasing.) After this "communion" we all kind of fell on the floor in a stupor. None of us could talk at all. Michelle, who had been my masseuse many times, started to massage my body. I could not feel a thing. I could not even feel her hands on my body, nor did I have any sense of them moving. I would have been frightened, but I knew better. I said, "Oh, I guess I am going through a re-organization of my DNA." That is the last thing I remember. I knew I would feel normal in the morning.

The next morning I was stunned that I had been blessed twice with this gift. I was convinced I would probably never even see the stuff again.

A year later I was at the home of Janice Kubo, another Saibaba devotee who was a student of mine. She had invited me to see the movies of Saibaba and how he materialized things to India. After the film I thanked her profusely. She suddenly invited me into her private temple room and offered me some more of the precious *Amrit*.

Another experience I had with Saibaba during those years involved the *vibuti*, the sacred ash he materializes. Michelle had just returned from her first trip to India and she was in a state of tremendous gratitude to me because I had cleared her mind and helped her to get herself to India free, she claimed, by the processes I had done on her during a Seattle LRT. I had not seen her for months — having been working on the East Coast — and so I did not know this.

Nor did I in the least suspect that, as I was flying toward Washington State, Mt. St. Helens was getting ready to erupt. I had, however, the day before, received a very unique letter from Robert. It said, "You are the highest woman I have ever met in the physical body. Please bring me an explosion. Love, Robert."

First of all, Robert never wrote letters, so I was shocked. And then I was doubly shocked by the last sentence. What did he mean . . . bring him an explosion?

That afternoon Michelle came to my hotel room, bringing me many pictures of Saibaba and spreading them all over the floor, saying I should pick one. I picked one that showed a large aura all around him. It was simply beautiful beyond words. Then she gave me a taste of the *vibuti*. It tasted like powdered perfume. I loved it. A sense of peace came over me immediately. I asked her if I could give some to Robert, as I knew he would come to my room that night. When he did, I showed him the picture of Saibaba. It was around four o'clock in the morning. He looked at it for a very long time without saying a word. He was spellbound. I said, "Well, since you are having that reaction, then I think it is right to give you a taste of this." We ate some together. I did not know that sometimes it has an effect of opening the throat chakra and making one be very expressive. I suddenly began screaming . . . I was erupting like a volcano! I yelled at him to get out and leave me alone. I had no idea what had come over me, nor did he. He left quite shocked. Everything I had ever suppressed came up in a flash. I did not want him to have to deal with it, so I made him leave. Then I cried, sure the relationship would be over because of that "scene." I simply could not understand what was going on. I never even got angry — let alone carry on with screaming! (Of course, I had no idea that the volcano nearby was about to go off for the first time in one hundred fifty years.)

The next morning my driver came at six to drive me to Portland, where I was to do the first LRT there that night. The whole thing was kind of a "fluke." Portland was not really ready for an LRT — we did not have enough rebirthers trained and I could not imagine having one there. There has not ever been one there since either. At about 11:30 we passed the site of Mt. St. Helens, but I didn't know it, nor did my driver. Apparently, the primary ash eruption occurred at that exact time! I was, however, still trying to integrate Saibaba's ash . . . I was feeling calm again, extremely calm, despite the fact my relationship might be over.

I settled into my room at the hotel in Portland. That night I turned on the TV and was very shocked to hear that Mt. St. Helens was about to go off several miles in the air for the first time in one hundred fifty to two hundred years! It was only forty miles from my window! It was late at night. I calmly dialed Robert's restaurant in Seattle. "Well Robert," I said, "you wanted me to bring you an explosion . . . Mt. St. Helens is exploding three miles in the air."

"Oh," he said calmly, "I think I'll have a little Beaujolais wine." He was sitting in his restaurant alone, all by himself as if waiting for this call. Neither of us had anything going on about the night before. It was as if it had never happened.

I was so calm I could not believe it. The next day I went to class as if nothing was going on. The volcano was continuing to erupt. The class probably would have panicked, but then they just moved smoothly right into my state of calmness. I said to them, "You see that mountain over there? The earth is trying to *rebirth* itself. We can no longer dump our negativity onto the earth. You must express yourself instead of stuffing it. You must open your throat chakras . . . you must breathe, you must clear yourselves." I did not really know what even I was saying. The next morning, however, the Sunday paper's head-lines said: "The Volcano is going through the opening of the throat chakra."

To this day I don't totally understand what all that was about. Could it be that Babaji and Saibaba and the masters sent me there to calm people down? Since I had gone through the mass hysteria the night before, I was able to do it. And so I carried around Saibaba's picture along with my pictures of my guru Babaji. I wondered what their relationship was like. More Saibaba devotees came to my classes. More of them brought me abundant amounts of *vibuti*, which I often used in ceremonies, giving *darshans* when I felt it was appropriate, or should I say, when I was so guided. It never occurred to me to go to South India to see Saibaba. I was one-thousand percent in-volved with trying to handle my teacher Babaji's impact on my life.

More and more I found myself thinking about Babaji, Jesus, and Saibaba together — and this was how my altar looked. They were together on my travelling altar. Sometimes people would come back with stories from Hherakhan saying that Babaji had sent Saibaba a letter. I thought that was unusual since they could obviously communicate telepathically. But I knew they must be playing games. And then I would go to North India to see Babaji, occasionally wondering if I should drop down to South India — to see Saibaba and finally meet him. But I would get so totally immersed in Hherakan and Babaji, that I would forget everything else on earth — and suddenly there would be no more time. One year, a Saibaba devotee came back to the States saying he had asked his guru, Saibaba, if he were really Babaji. Saibaba had apparently replied, "No, I am not Babaji . . . but Babaji has a very immense mission." It was apparently said with tremendous respect. I was pleased, imagining how they must somehow be working together . . . just like the LRT trainers worked together, our different personalities resulting in different missions, different types of situations that attracted different types of students.

One thing I had always loved about Babaji was that he would never speak negatively about another guru. He would never force us to wear one certain color just to indicate we belonged to him. In fact, sometimes he would send us to other gurus to straighten us out. It would make things easier on him. It seemed intelligent to me. So, I never felt guilty thinking about Saibaba, who once said:

"Cows may be different in breeds or color or size, but the milk they yield is the same the world over. So, too, all religions, whatever their origin, are all means to the same God."

Therefore, at the first God Training in Mt. Shasta, which I had dedicated to Babaji and created as a result of his request, the altar for the class remained with several pictures of different masters. During that second week of spiritual purification, I suddenly made the decisions to go back to India, take a group with me, and meet Saibaba. I was, after all, overdue to go back to India. India had always been, and will always be, a huge *stretch* for me. She herself, no matter what guru I met there, processed me, hurled me to new levels of consciousness, and moved me through decades of learning in a week or two. I did not dare think about the hardships, the struggle getting there, the hassles, the difficulty traveling, the trials one had to go through, the austerity of the ashrams, the cleansing required. If I had, I may have resisted. I made the decision and asked Dennis if he would go with me. He prayed that night for six hours. The next morning he said, "I am going with you to India." The trip was on. Once you tell another, you keep your word . . . or so it was with me.

Next I told my colleague Loy. We decided to go for it all the way. We would do another version of the "God Training" on the road. Why not invite Terry Cole and make it a real experience in networking, which was our latest assignment anyway? Weren't we going to learn how to get groups to-gether?

My good friend D.C. Cordoba came back into my life about that time. She had chosen Saibaba as her guru two years before, when her mother had been healed by him in a dream. I asked her if she would organize the trip . . . as neither Loy nor Terry nor myself had a speck of time for that. I had no idea what it would be like to take a group with us. It did seem like the right thing to do for many reasons. On my first trip to India, Leonard had taken a small group of us along with him, and I remember how grateful I was to not have gone alone the first time. I wanted to give others the opportunity I had had.

D.C. began to plan the trip immediately. She amazed us at her ability to get it all together on such short notice. The only time we could all go was early February. I remembered that gurus often travel about India in February, so I had a bit of concern whether Saibaba would be at his ashram or not. D.C. was not the least bit concerned. She seemed certain the whole time.

I was willing to take the risk even though I had to also risk the disappointment of seventy-eight people who were sud-denly going with us. Days and days later we were on a very hot, dusty bus ride with this group. The air conditioning had burned out long ago and everyone was quite exhausted. I wondered how the group would hold up, having never been to India nor having experienced the austerities of an ashram. They were taken to a large hall, which they later called the "barn," and given the cement floor. D.C. and I ran to the temple, tired as we were, hoping to catch an early glimpse of

Saibaba. Just as we got there, a new red Mercedes drove up and he got out. How thrilling. We thought he always arrived in a new Mercedes each day. It was only later we found out that he had just *then* returned from an India tour and had been gone for twenty whole days before our arrival. Had we arrived a week sooner we would have missed him completely. What timing!

I always have so much to say, yet when I see a real guru, I am speechless. Nothing seems good enough. Usually my reaction is, at the first glimpse: "Just this moment, just this glimpse was worth the whole trip. Anything after this is sheer gravy."

The ashram was very large compared to what I was used to in the Himalayas. I was very impressed with the way he handled the masses, something I very much wanted to learn from him. Many "groups" were trying to get his attention. The group from Argentina was all dressed alike wearing soft green cotton saris. They always came to temple together, dressed alike and very much in unison. They were very determined to get a private *darshan*. Our group, mostly Californians, didn't seem to be able to get it together at first to look alike nor make it to the temple at the same time. We finally got pink bandannas, however, and sometimes we got organized enough to meet under the monkey tree in a group of about thirty. Saibaba called the Argentines "Urgentines." I didn't want our group to be so urgent so I didn't push things.

Every day in the afternoon we would have meetings and lectures. Terry would film for her ministry classes under the meditation tree between *darshans* in the morning. In the afternoon Loy and I would lecture between *darshans*. Every other day we would have a group rebirth in the "barn." About the fourth day Saibaba materialized some *vibuti* for some of the men in our group. Everyone began affirming that he would take us in for a private *darshan*.

At night is when I felt he worked on me the most. I would have dreams of my childhood and past. Clearing and clearing.

I prayed to him to be able to complete every little remnant of my father's death forever.

I was pleased how well the group did. Very few got sick, and, of course, I attribute this partly to the rebirthings we did and the classes between *darshans*. We divided the group into smaller groups and assigned a group leader to each small group. This worked very well. The week went incredibly fast . . . we only had one day left. The night before the last day we received word that he would see the "Americans" for a private *darshan* the next day. Everyone in our group was wild with excitement. That night in my room, D.C., my attendant Annahit, and myself all had dreams about sex! Everyone dressed up the next morning in pretty saris. When he finally said "The Americans," there was a real stir.

We were called into the side temple . . . everyone crowding to get close to him. I touched his feet, which, it was said, clears lifetimes of karma. Everyone held up their letters, praying he would take them. (If he does, it is like a "yes" to your requests.) He immediately materialized a silver locket for the man who was least popular in the group. The group had been quite judgmental (including myself) for this man's very inappropriate crazy behavior. Saibaba started with him loving him so much. Then he started giving us a lecture. I have no clue as to what he really said, but it was quite divine, to put it mildly. Everyone seemed to be moving into an altered state, many began sobbing and going into spontaneous rebirths, as he pulled us in closer and closer.

He would often suddenly interrupt himself, quickly reading someone's mind or asking them a question or noticing something about them. Once he suddenly asked Dennis if he wanted his golden nugget ring "changed." Of course Dennis said yes and handed it to him. Saibaba blew on it and transformed it into a totally different ring with his own picture on it. This was perfect for Dennis, who has always been studying how to do such things and who has himself the ability as a healer to perform etheric surgery and do reorganizing of body cells. Everyone was getting antsy and pushing for something. He kept saying, "Wait! Wait! Don't haste!" He finally took my letter. I had waited patiently all week for that, patience never having been one of my virtues. For once, I didn't force it to make it happen. It happened at the end. He gave me so much energy in that last moment that I was instantly in a rebirthing.

Finally, he gave us all *vibuti* and allowed Terry's TV cameras to roll. He gave us a long time with him. People said later that that was rare. We were in bliss. All of us were in bliss. He told us he was always with us and would not disappoint us.

"I am the Repairer of Broken Hearts, damaged minds, diseased feelings, twisted fancies. I am the Smith who welds, mends and molds," he once said. Surely, that was our experience that last day. Later, when we all shared under the meditation tree with Terry about our experiences, we heard many beautiful reports of miracles. One woman in our group had gone up to him and told him she had a lump in her breast. Later when she finally had the courage, she touched the area, and it had disappeared!

Thank you! Thank you, Saibaba.

Thank you for sending us Mailea to guide our whole trip. Thank you for your Grace, Saibaba. We love you. We want to serve you.

Jesus

Jesus was my childhood teacher. There is no doubt that He gave me my entire spiritual foundation, through Christianity. I was raised as a Lutheran, American Lutheran, to be exact. I was baptized, went to Sunday School, Bible School, Confirmation School, and was confirmed a Lutheran. I even went to a Lutheran College my first year. I became, however, very confused after my father died. He was a very religious man, and when he died, they said, "The Lord took him away." I could not resolve this. I could not understand how the Lord, who was supposed to be loving, killed people. This was intolerable to me.

Soon after that, I rejected the church. Christianity suddenly did not work for me, and I completely stopped thinking about Jesus and suppressed my love for Him. I was wounded. Later, after marrying an atheist out of rebellion and anger at God, I found that my temporary happiness was again crushed. I went through a divorce. I was again very, very wounded. Once after my divorce, I tried to go back to church. It was, however, entirely too emotional, and I cried during the service so much that I left early. Years later, after re-entering the spiritual life by finding rebirthing, I began to get healed. I began to open up to Jesus again — but just a little. Then a friend told me about the

Course in Miracles and boldly sent me the first chapter photo-copied so that I could not avoid it. I began to study the books which were clearly written by Jesus. I felt quite healed by the books, but the first year I still had resistance and did not surrender completely.

Once my sister confronted me about having given up all my former convictions. Once my mother confronted me when I told her I had found the *Course*. She tried to tell me it was in direct contradiction to the teachings of Jesus. I tried to tell her the books were written *by* Jesus. We had an argument. I cried. I was shocked that my intention was on the one hand to show her that I was going back to Jesus and the result turned out just the opposite of what I had hoped. It seemed that the only way I was going to have any kind of relationship with my own blood family was if I stuck only to my childhood religion. This did not work for me. I remained torn apart. I had only begun to recover from the confusion of my childhood with the help of rebirthing and finally my true guru Babaji. Only there had I found clarity and peace of mind.

On my second trip to India, I had been deeper into the *Course in Miracles* by then, deeper into rebirthing, and deeper into my guru. My mother was still having a hard time with that, asking me how I could resolve my relationship with Babaji with my relationship with Jesus. I tried to explain to her that they were all one and I saw no separation. This did not seem to appease her. I knew I was going to shave my head on this trip to India. I decided not to tell her until after it was done.

My last day with Babaji on that trip I decided to ask him for help on this matter. I remember climbing the one hundred eight steps from the Ganges up to the ashram. I was going to leave the next day. So I finally asked him telepathically how I could explain this matter to my mother. That night he gave me a dream.

In the dream, I was moving to a new house. I liked the house very much and I wanted to rent it very much, and I told the landlord so. "There is only one thing," he said. "This house comes complete with a roommate, and you have to take it that way or not at all." "Who is that?" I asked. "You will see after you decide," he replied. Apparently, I could not find out until after I said yes. This was taking a big chance, but I wanted the house very much, so I said yes. Somehow I trusted him. The next day I moved in, very curious to see who my roommate would be. I went to the other bedroom next to mine and there He was. It was Jesus. He appeared to me full on. Glowing. Alive in all his radiance. Jesus was to be my new roommate. I awoke in bliss, preparing to leave the ashram. Later I told my mother the dream. She never confronted me again. Somehow my mother has been very clear about my work ever since and very supportive.

Later, when Babaji asked me to do the God Training, I decided to go to Bali and try to meditate on what that meant. The main reading material I took was the *Course in Miracles*. It was my third year trying to study it. Sometimes I would remember that was Jesus talking to me. Sometimes I would forget. The first year I studied those books I had a lot of resistance and I would go unconscious a lot (ego). The second year I would say to myself, "This is starting to make a lot of sense to me." The third year in Bali I ended up saying, "This is the *only* thing that makes sense to me." I read the books every day. I outlined the text hours and hours. This took me six weeks. All I can say is this: I was in bliss studying the words of Jesus. Partly it was because I was in the energy of Bali, but mostly it was because I allowed myself to be, once again, in the energy of Jesus.

After Bali, I had to put the manuscript away as I was "too busy." That was my ego again, of course. Apparently, that was all the bliss I could handle for awhile. It was not until nine months later, when I went to St. Martins island in the Caribbean, to finish writing the book *Drinking the Divine* that I was able to get back to that state of bliss. Again, I worked on the book (energy of Jesus) every day for two weeks. I was in constant bliss again. I went away with so much power, so much bliss, that I was able to accomplish incredible amounts of work, incomprehensible to people around me.

I acknowledge the energy of Jesus and the perfection of Jesus as total bliss. I pray that I can learn to handle it and stay in it. I pray that people will be inspired to study the *Course in Miracles*. I pray that I can serve Jesus because he has completed his part perfectly, he has laid out the plan for all of us, and all we have to do is follow it. I pray that I will learn to integrate the *Course* and teach it. I pray that the God Training will further this goal beyond my imagination. I pray that I can serve Jesus by teaching the *Course*.

My friend, Ken Wapnick, the world's leading expert on the *Course*, has said that the *Course* is the most important work in two thousand years. I would agree. Ken also made the statement that the presence of Jesus on the planet brought up so much ego that it has taken two thousand years to process it. Now after processing that, we are ready for the next step, and that is the *Course*. If I had a prayer for the world, it would be that everyone could be exposed to the clarity and healing of His words in the *Course*. The answers are there. The way is there.

I pray that I could inspire people to read it.

Finding My True Guru

🦅

Shiva Mahavatar Babaji, known to hundreds of thousands in the world through Paramahansa Yogananda's book, *Autobiography of a Yogi*, appeared in June 1970 in a cave that had been holy for thousands of years at the foot of the Mt. Kailash. Being a mahavatar, or human manifestation of God, he was not born of a woman.

He has no known parents or family, appearing first as a youth of eighteen or so and displaying great wisdom and power. Some Hairakhan villagers saw him as an old man with a long white beard. Others saw him as a young man with no beard. Two men spoke to him at the same time and one saw an old man with a beard and the other saw a young man with no beard. He was also seen at different places at the same time. He knew the scriptures and could quote them in Sanskrit as well as in Hindi, yet there is no evidence of his being educated. He ate almost nothing for months on end, up to two or three years, and his energy was boundless.

Late in September 1970, he walked to the top of Mt. Kailash with a small group of men and seated himself in a Yogi-fashion in a small temple there. He sat like this for fourty-five days without leaving his seat and without eating, drinking, or sleeping. After that, hundreds came to celebrate the nine day religious festival of Navratri with him.

His coming had been foretold both by ancient scriptures and by the preaching and prophesying of a twentieth-century Indian Saint called Mahendra Baba. For many years he went around India, preaching that Babaji would return to transform the world by changing the hearts and minds of men. He described what Babaji would look like, including the scars on his right leg and left arm and said that Babaji would come in 1970.

There are books in Hindi written about the previous manifestation of Hairakhan Baba, which lasted from 1800 to 1922. Around the year 1800, he appeared to villagers not far from Hherakhan out of a ball of light. And, in 1922, before a handful of followers, he disappeared into a ball of light. There are many recorded miracles — healing people, restoring the dead to life, feeding multitudes from a small portion of food, changing his form, being in two or more places at one time, etc. On two or three occasions Babaji said he was one of the teachers of Jesus Christ.

In order to focus people's minds on God, Babaji taught people to repeat the ancient mantra *Om Namaha Shivaya*. It is a Sanskrit phrase which means: "I surrender to bow to/take refuge in God." The main purpose of Shri Babaji's coming in human manifestation was to reform the hearts and minds of men. He came to remove confusion and evil from mankind. Babaji taught that all should lead lives based on truth, love, and simplicity. He said over and over that Karma yoga, (unselfish work dedicated to God) is the best, easiest and most rewarding fastest way to God in this chaotic, confused era of change. Service to humanity is our first duty.

Meeting Babaji

So there I was in New Delhi, feeling really alone, with Leonard having told me to meet him up north and Abubabaji telling me to stay with him. I was like glue for those three days. I finally could not stand it anymore. The only solution was to scream, which I did; hoping to get myself unstuck. At midnight I went outside and yelled at God, "I demand to know which is the right spiritual path for me." I screamed, "And furthermore, I demand to know tonight in a dream!" That night I had a dream alright. I saw Hairakhan up in the foothills of the Himalayas where Leonard had gone. I heard the music. I did not see Babaji, just the music was enough. The next morning, very early, I was at the bus station. An Indian bus station could be the worst. I was mildly horrified at it but yet excited. The bus ride was at first horrible. I was packed in there with peasants, pigs, and chickens. I had to sit on a tire for ten straight hours. The woman in front of me was vomiting the whole time. Fortunately, I had been through the Peace Corps. I could handle it. I lost myself in my books. I reviewed the part about Babaji in the *Autobiography of a Yogi* (Chapters 33 and 34) and the only other book available on him, a little black book called *Hherakhan Known and Unknown*. I started going into absolute bliss. It was like he was pulling me in his aura. It was fantastic.

We were dropped off at a little town called Haldwani. It was late, and we found a raunchy hotel with mattresses, no sheets. Next morning, I set out to find this man Muniraj, the Saint who supposedly checked you out and approved you for the rest of the trip to the ashram. The whole thing was kind of a struggle — I was still into struggles that year. It took me four hours to find him. I kept asking people in the streets and kept getting no response. But I did not give up. I figured it was a test. The fourth hour, someone led me down a street. Finally, I found Muniraj at a feed store. He was the first person connected to Baba I ever met. He was simply beautiful, seemed to me the most peaceful man on earth. I melted. My harshness started going. He nodded and led me to a path. There were a few of us hiking together now which was nice. It wasn't so easy with backpacks as we had to cross the swift Ganges river eight or ten times. It was knee-deep and we had to stop and take our shoes off. In fact it was quite an ordeal. It never occurred to me to hire a donkey or a porter that first year, as I did in later years. Like I say, I was still into struggling. I nearly fell over several times and once I did get my shoes soaking wet. After a few hours, I looked up and there it was! The ashram up on a hill, exactly like I had seen in the dream! The valley was beautiful. There were bananas and lush plants all around the temple up there. And over on the other side was Jeannie, Leonard's girlfriend, with her head painted in funny stripes.

"What are you doing over here by yourself . . . why aren't you up in the temple?" I asked her. "Because I have my period . . . I have to stay over here by myself for five days." I had a *fit*. I couldn't believe there was such a ridiculous rule. I suddenly felt like I was a hard core woman's libber. No way were they ever going to get *me* to be banned from anywhere just because I was a woman! Good thing my period wasn't due. What a ridiculous rule.

Then I saw the one hundred eight steps leading up to the ashram. I forgot about what I had just felt and seen. I ran up those steps with incredible energy, passing a "peasant" who was sitting at the top. He had a piece of straw hanging out of his mouth.

"Hey," someone said, grabbing my skirt. "You are supposed to *pranam* to the Guru."

"Well, where is he?" I asked. Having *no idea* what I was looking for. After all, we had had no pictures.

"Over there," this person said, pointing to the "peasant."

I simply could not believe it was him. I had expected silk robes. What a shock! I kneeled down and his first words to me were "Oh, MRS. Sondra!" What did he mean, MRS. Sondra? How did he know my name!

Babaji told me to go to my room and rest. I was given an empty room with one or two others. It wasn't so bad. On the way to my room I had passed Leonard. He nodded, hardly able to speak. He looked weird. His forehead was also painted with colored stripes. I laid down to rest. Almost immediately hundreds of huge black flies attacked me. It was my first test. They absolutely were not on anyone else. I must have had terrible resistance. They would not go away. "I can't stay in this place," I cried. It was an awful feeling. Fortunately, Daru came in, a doctor from America, reminding me that I had just gotten there and I had not given this place a chance. He was kind enough to read to me for a half hour from the *Course in Miracles*, which I had had in my backpack. Heavy as they were, it was perfect I lugged them up there. My mind finally snapped, and the flies left. Got through that one.

So then I got up, trying to find my way around the ashram and see what the routine was. I immediately started my period; and of course it was not time at all for that breakthrough bleeding. I was horrified. No way was I going to sit across the river for days. I had no time or patience for that. Furthermore, I had come thousands of miles to be in the temple with Babaji. I went to Leonard for help. "What about this rule you can't to in the temple if you have your period, Leonard?"

"Don't ask me, Sondra! I have my own problems over here," he said. He seemed out of it, too.

I sat in the corner trying to meditate, trying to work out a plan. I finally decided I should try self esteem. If Babaji was who he said he was, he knew everything. He knew then that I had started my period at the wrong time, and he also knew then my *intense burning desire* to be in the temple with him and everyone. There had to be a way I could participate without breaking the rules. I suddenly had a brainstorm. I would sit outside the temple and that way I could see him and hear the music. After all, it was an open air temple. And that way I wouldn't be breaking the rules exactly since I was not inside. And that way I would not be left out. It seemed like a daring plan. I knew I was really on my own with it, but I was willing to take the risk and see what happened.

The bells rang for temple. I felt brave. Across the courtyard came Babaji, just as I was about to leave my room. He was

dressed as I had dreamed — in satin robes with a turban! Later
it occurred to me he might have greeted me at the top of the
steps wearing farmer's clothes since I was raised with farmers.
I mean, after all, I never saw him greet others that way, nor did
I see him sit on the top of the steps like that waiting for
someone with straw in his mouth. He began to play the
fashion game with me, believe it or not. I loved clothes.

Babaji looked right at me very intensely from about fifty
feet away. It was my first direct contact with him. He threw his
satin robe over his shoulder just like I always throw my shawls
over my shoulder. But he gave me such an intense look that I
literally fell over. I remember thinking as I was falling that I
better start praying. I was suddenly saying, "Dear God, let me
surrender to this man!" I also remembered Leonard's other
departing words when he had left for the mountains without
me. He was chiding me, "You think you are so smart Sondra.
Babaji is going to have your case in one second!" Yes, well, that
had scared me a bit. And here it was. I picked myself up off the
ground, now wondering if I should go ahead with my daring
plan after *that*! Well, I did it. I sat right outside the temple.
Everyone was chanting. Babaji was up on his throne. It was
exciting and scary. I sat there on the ground and sat there, very
relieved that I was allowed to stay. I did not understand
anything about the place. The chanting was in Sanskrit. All I
knew was I did not want to be away from Babaji. He was the
most amazing thing I had ever seen in my life.

Suddenly I heard someone yell loudly, "Stop!" My God, it
was Babaji. He had ordered everyone to stop chanting. Then I
heard him yell, "You!" I couldn't believe it. He was actually
yelling at me! This was the dreaded moment. Would I have to
leave? But then he raised his hand, motioning me to come in
instead. What a miracle. He let me in! I rushed in and sat
down. I was thrilled. The chanting resumed. I was ecstatic,
feeling victory. My plan had worked. Suddenly, however, I
heard him yell, "Stop!" once again. And then he looked right at
me. Everyone in the whole place turned and looked right at

me. It was very intense to say the least. "Are you a man or woman?" he shouted. (Why was he always shouting?) "I am a woman!" I insisted. (God, couldn't he tell?)

"Well then, sit over there!" he remarked. He pointed to the other side where the women were. In my haste I had not noticed that the women were sitting separately. I had not even noticed that I was sitting with the men. Leonard was right. In one second, he had me down to my case. (At my birth I was sure I should have been a boy in order to please everyone.) I was shaking. I moved over with the women. The chanting started again, went on for awhile. Then I heard him once again shouting, "Stop!" Oh no, I couldn't take another blasting. I braced myself. This time he let me alone, but he threw out three other Americans . . . females . . . rebirthers . . . told them to go to the fire house. Apparently, he did not want to bother with their energy? I was curious why he threw them out. I couldn't get it off my mind. Maybe they were shivering? I was cold too. It was December. We had to be wrapped in blankets.

❧

Time for *darshan*. We were to go up in front and kneel before him and have a blessing. If you are new, it is the time you bring him a gift. I had brought him a fancy elaborate candle that when lit, formed many rainbows all over the room. I saw him give everyone's gifts away as soon as he received them. I had heard he would do this; but then I wanted to be special. I wanted him to keep mine for his room. I placed it at his feet, received my *darshan* and sat down while the others continued in the line. To my amazement, he put the candle to his side, seemingly enjoying it. It was the only thing he kept. I was thrilled. But then at the end, he drove me nuts by giving it to the person in the room I disliked the most. Of course, another lesson. Constant lessons here.

I kept wondering about the other American girls. I couldn't stand it. I had to know where they were sent to. I really gathered up my nerve and went right up to Babaji at the end of the temple and said I wanted to see where he had sent them. "Besides, I am cold," I acknowledged, "And I would like permission to go to the fire myself."

"Fine," he replied while he passed Leonard some brandy to loosen him up. Brandy? What kind of place was this anyway? I did not understand anything. Neither did Leonard.

I went to the little fire house adjoining the temple. I could not believe what I saw in there. There was the sacred fire and there were about eight very old, and I mean *very* old, Saints sitting around the fire. The three American girls were in between them. They seemed to be oblivious to my arrival. I wondered if they were in some kind of trance. A very old man motioned for me to come and sit next to him. I found out later his name was Prem Baba. He was very cuddly and somehow extremely "sexy." He *seemed* to be somewhere between ninety-nine years old and two hundred ninety-nine years old. How could he be so sexy? He began to sing to me as if I was the only woman on earth. Was this my welcome finally to the ashram? Had I passed the tests? He began to pass me a kind of peace-pipe, wanting me to take a smoke. I looked up. All the old men nodded. This was some kind of ritual I was obviously supposed to do in there. The other girls had taken it obviously, so I thought I better. I did not understand how to smoke the thing. You had to draw it in through the hands in some complicated fashion. Prem Baba was trying to teach me. He held it for me. I had to suck the smoke in through his hands. It was a bit too sexy for me, the whole thing. I finally did it, trying to get into the swing of things. I was immediately soaring, way out be-yond everything. I must have gone in an altered state really fast . . . everything became very romantic to me. Prem Baba was like my absolute wonderful lover, still singing to me. I asked someone what he was singing. The old men said "All he ever talks about is God." Well God was very romantic that night.

My first night at the ashram was surely a surprise. I wondered if that was really Babaji in another body sitting next to me. I knew he could be in several bodies at once. I didn't know what to make of anything. I must have left my body, because the next thing I remember was the old men slapping me hard on the back. I came crashing in. Then I decided that that was enough for my first night. I asked Fan if she would walk me to my room, which she did, thank God.

I got in my sleeping bag, thinking I was going to sleep. Babaji suddenly appeared to be floating over my sleeping bag in a baby's body with an old man's head! I recognized the head as being one of his from his earlier materialization in the 1920s. This was quite astonishing. Unlike other visions that come and go rapidly, this one stayed right there all night and would not disappear. The "light" was overwhelming. I started to tremble. I was soon shaking — a lot! I could not stop. I finally called out to my friend the doctor to come. Would he please get a flashlight and read to me from the *Course* again? I was terrified of that much energy. He was wonderful, reading to me by flashlight the words of Jesus until I calmed down. The vision remained right there in front of me all night. I did not sleep at all.

The next morning after temple Babaji called us all down to meet on the banks of the Ganges, somewhere near the cave where he materialized his body. (Believe it or not, my first year at the ashram, I was so freaked out, I did not even go to the cave, not even once. I did not even see the entrance.) There we were, the morning of my first full day at the ashram, a few Americans, a few Germans, a few Dutch, a few Italians. It seemed like only about thirty of us. I was barely holding it together. Suddenly Baba said, "You!" pointing to me.

"Oh no," I thought, not again.

He called me "You" for three days. "You," he shouted, "Give a speech. You're a teacher."

A speech? I could not believe it. A speech by the Ganges? About what? I had to get it together fast. "Well," I thought, "It is like the LRT. I'll share." And so I stood up and shared my experience from the night before. Everyone seemed pretty interested; but, of course, I wondered if I was doing it right. I glanced out the corner of my eye at Babaji to check out his reaction. He was there, but not there. He seemed to be on other planets at the same time. But there he was, actually coloring in a book like a five-year-old! He was always like a child and a two thousand-year-old man at the same time. He was always there and other places at the same time. He was always right inside of you and right inside of everyone else in a different way at the same time. If you asked others their experience, you would never know they had been there at the same time.

Got through that. Guess I did okay. The new people were told to meet him back up in the garden near the temple. I knew he was going to tell us how long we could stay. I had heard stories that he often sent people away the minute they got there or only let some stay one day. Some people could only handle a few minutes of his presence, I had heard. I was bracing myself. I really wanted to stay two weeks, the full time of my visa. But what if he told me to leave now? He sat us all in a circle, me on the left. "You can stay two days," he said to that one. "You can stay four days," he said to the next one. "You leave tomorrow," he said to the next . . . and on and on. I couldn't believe I had to wait until last. He told each new person their exact time of stay. I was shaking, preparing myself for the worst. Suddenly he looked at me. It was my turn. Was he going to yell "You" again? Would I have to leave tomorrow?

He turned to me, and much to my great surprise, in the most gentle loving voice he asked, "How long would you like to stay?"

I could not believe it. "Two weeks is all I can stay," I replied. "Okay," he said.

He would speak to me in Hindi, but it seemed to be immediately translated into English somehow in my mind. How did that happen? I was so happy. I could stay the full time I wanted, and I could have stayed even longer had I had the right visa! What a miracle.

From then on he treated me totally differently. He treated me with so much respect, so much love. And that night he even gave me a name. At *darshan* he leaned over and said, "Your name: *Durkuley*."

I asked for a translation from his assistant. "It means strong one, immortal, everlasting," she replied. I was *really* happy. I could not imagine a more perfect name! (Later I was told that it also means: "Cosmic Space Traveler.") And so we went deep into the ashram life: Up at 4 A.M. in the dark. Down to bathe in the cold Ganges in the dark. Meditation. Early morning temple . . . chanting the Aarti for hours. *Darshan*. Tea at the little shack on the hill. Karma yoga . . . work down by the river . . . usually carrying rocks. Lunch served from pails onto "plates" made of leaves sewn together. Washing clothes in the river. Siesta. Karma yoga . . . building bridges. Afternoon chants in the garden with Baba. Dinner, again served from pails onto leaves . . . no utensils. Temple in the evening . . . chanting the Aarti for hours. *Darshan*.

Soon each one of us got into our own particular paranoia. It was all very intense. It didn't take long to get "plugged in" by his presence along with the chanting four to five hours every day. I soon became completely paranoid about food. It wasn't that I was worried about the food making me sick. I was suddenly paranoid about all food in the world, having been poisoned in a past life; and having been born on the kitchen table in this life. I could not function. I soon became obsessed and a complete nervous wreck over food. I imagined I was gaining kilos and kilos daily. I felt bloated, full, wanting to vomit. I was a wreck. I finally went up to Baba in the garden.

"I am a nervous wreck about food," I confessed.

He suddenly got up, towering over me and said, "Give up food."

My god, I thought. He wants me to become a breatharian, a Saint like Anna Lee Skarin and Theresa Newman who lived on communion wafers.

"Right now?" I asked.

"No, no. You eat this food. Ashram food holy. You wait until America. When you go back, you give up food."

I began to imagine never eating again in the States. During temple I would sit there, trying to chant, but seeing apparitions of food instead. Steaks would go by, floating in mid air, sizzling, smelling fantastic. The worst was pizzas. Fabulous pizzas would float by, my favorite food. I would go mad. I could not stand it any more. Finally, I kneeled before him crying. "Babaji, I have gone crazy," I confessed. "I cannot chant, I cannot meditate, I cannot pray, I cannot think. I am completely crazy now around food. Please help me." I begged him. He took pity on me. Suddenly he picked up these huge steel Army band cymbals and crashed them over my head. The sound and vibration roared through my body. Everything disappeared. I felt clear, suddenly clear. Later it occurred to me that I had not seen the cymbals there before that moment nor ever after. He must have materialized those things. They were huge! The treatment worked.

And so on I went, trying to hold it together. I was, however, slowly crumbling. My ego had had it. Babaji would drive me wild with sudden sweeping statements out of nowhere. One day he walked up to me in the garden and said, "You and Leonard think you are so smart. Go handle L.A. and then I will be impressed." *Los Angeles?* I didn't know anyone in L.A. nor did I want to be there. I tried not to think about it. But I did. What did he mean *handle* L.A.? Another time he came up and whispered in my ear. "I'll meet you in Washington."

❧

Once he announced in temple that if we wanted to have immortality, we should stay up all night that night and meditate on the bonfire which would be down by the river. Naturally, I thought everyone would go. Only a few of us did, which shocked me. Didn't they hear? Didn't they want it? It began to rain. First test. Well, I went anyway. A huge fire was built. I looked at it roar. About three o'clock I got a little sleepy and started to fall over. An old man came around with a stick and poked at me, telling me to shape up and get busy saying the chants.

Babaji had been mad at Italy that day. He was blasting the Italians for being so irresponsible. He had thrown half of them out and had sent others off to somewhere down the river. I was wondering what was going on with Italy. Suddenly an Italian girl he had sent to the woods came stumbling up to the fire site. She was acting *crazy*. She had taken some kind of drug. Apparently this drug was driving her really crazy and she had been on it three days! It was apparently some local plant. I was trying to meditate on the fire, but she suddenly came and sat down in front of me and began to eat *rocks*! I was more than horrified. All my nursing stuff came up in one swoop. No one had ever died in my presence, not even when I was a nurse. Did it have to happen now? Why was he putting this crazy woman in front of me who couldn't even speak English? I was panicked! Would she get perforated intestines and die right in front of me while I was meditating on physical immortality? I was told not to move all night, but shouldn't I be doing *something*? Was I having a hallucination? I was not on drugs. But then I felt like I would go crazy! I remember thinking: Babaji has placed her in front of me for a reason. I have to sit here and watch all the insanity of the ego.

Fortunately, there was a miracle. Muniraj's mother was sitting next to me. She suddenly picked up this Italian girl and took off all her clothes. Then she began to massage her and chanted over her. She massaged her for hours, restoring her to sanity. Quite a thing I had to go through that night. What a lesson. I saw insanity restored to sanity with love only. Love did it.

I barely recovered from that. The next morning, Babaji came up to me and said, "You go for walk with me."

I followed him. We walked along the Ganges and he began to speak to me in perfect English. It was then that I remembered that he could speak any language at any time if he wanted to. He led me up the river to a warehouse. It was there he had sent the Italians he had banned from the temple. They were instructed to clean up the place, which was filthy. Apparently Babaji was not happy with the job they did. He began screaming at this one guy and suddenly picked him up and threw him against the wall! I was horrified! I never could handle anger (which is exactly why Babaji made me go along to witness that scene). I could not *imagine* the guru getting angry. I ran out of the room crying. I sat on the edge of the cliff overlooking the Ganges sobbing. Babaji came out and stood over me. He suddenly reached under his robes and pulled out a Hershey bar with almonds. He was laughing. Lesson over. I became convinced he made up the whole scene for me. I was going to have to learn to handle anger in my space.

On this trip I brought along about twenty-five LRT red ceramic hearts to give to Babaji. I thought he might give them out to the children. After giving them to him, I asked if I could pin one on his garment and he let me do that. Then he proceeded to give them out to various devotees who kneeled before him. The next day everyone seemed to be wearing these hearts. There seemed to be a lot more around than I had brought. I was going to go about counting them all to see if I was imagining it or not, but then so many things happened I forgot all about it. That night Babaji came in wearing his heart upside down. Then everyone turned theirs upside down. I could not figure out why he was doing this. It was some kind of little joke on me to drive me nuts. It really *did* keep my mind busy.

That first year I didn't even notice people shaving their heads. I didn't notice a lot of things. I was just trying to make it through, second by second. I could not even chant. I would just sit in the temple hoping to *absorb* the chants. It was better than trying to follow along. I could never follow along. I would lose my place constantly. You might say I had a hard time.

Some of my friends had an even harder time. None of us were doing so hot. Just when we though we might collapse and die or something, Baba would come over and knock us with a stick or something — and we would go into bliss. Once I remember I was feeling pretty awful. My back was hurting. I was trying to eat lunch. Baba came up behind me and hit me in the exact place my back hurt. I was instantly healed. Suddenly he was up on top of the roof throwing white doves on me. I didn't see any ladders or any way he got up there.

My wealthy Japanese friend, Steve, was there at the ashram also that year. He had come at my insistence and had brought his young son, who he was very attached to. He was having no easy time either.

The first thing Baba said to him was, "You leave your son here in India and take this dog home with you . . ."

Steve went nuts over that because he was overly attached to his son and he had a tremendous charge on dogs due to a painful childhood incident. Of course after several days Baba "changed his mind" and Steve was off the hook. Steve had barely recovered from that when Baba sent him off along to Haldwin one night for film. Steve was gone for days. When he came back, he told me tales of how he had been freezing in the streets. Being a wealthy millionaire, he got "processed" on gratitude. One night he ended up confronted by an old leper woman in the street who really took him through it. She kept asking him over and over if he would trade places with her. Later he realized Baba had taken over her body.

᠅

We all went through really hard times that first year because we all had so much ego and he was pushing us to the limit.

Steve, Dharu, the doctor, and myself left the ashram together that time — relieved we had survived and totally in love with Baba. We knew that even though it was rough, he had saved us decades and decades of time in our healing process. I thought I would be smart and go back by donkey. Well, I jumped on my donkey and took off. Before I knew it I had to face the next trial: My billfold and all IDs had just "disappeared." I had to let go. My identity was apparently totally changed. Then we had to face a hail storm. I actually got under my burro. We finally got out of the valley to a truck packed with peasants. By the time we got to the bus station, it was freezing cold at night. I remember freezing the whole way. I was congratulating myself, however, because I had remembered to reserve a deluxe room at the Oberoi Hotel in Delhi — and I was promising my friends a hot shower and fresh sheets. I told them I'd share my room with them.

The room was beautiful, but the minute we all stepped into it, we all three became violently ill with vomiting and diarrhea. We all felt like we were dying. I remember we would take turns crawling into the bathroom. I finally just laid on the floor by the bathroom. Forget the sheets. I was too sick to care. On top of that, Dhara had a "Dear John letter" waiting for him at the Oberoi. He was given the news that his fiancee had run off with his best friend! He wanted to kill himself. I remember him calling out to me to please crawl over to the other side of the room and help him. I called out, too sick to move, "Dharu, I wish I could help you, but I am dying, too." We were a disaster, the three of us.

We had to be at the airport at 8 A.M. At 7 A.M. we were suddenly and mysteriously healed all at once. What a cleansing! At least it didn't happen on the bus! Wow, were we grateful for that.

※

Toward the end of my second year after meeting him, he gave me one of the highest experiences of all my lifetimes. He showed me I could dematerialize and rematerialize. I know he gave me that experience so that I would have certainty that I was teaching the truth. It was the most glorious moment of my life. And it happened in Washington. It took me several years to recover from that. I couldn't even talk about it. Even yet, I have only written a very little about it. I don't feel ready. Some things are definitely way beyond words, at least my words, at least this time.

Leonard was brave enough to go back to India the next year. He came back with his head shaved. He was really on me about doing that. I was resisting going back; but then the exact amount of money to go came to me as a gift. So I knew it was time. I asked Phil to go along. I really wanted to be with another rebirther. (Thank God I was smart enough to plan ahead.) Leonard was staying at our house. It was about nine days before we were to go.

"I want you to shave your head, Sondra," he said. I told him I was resisting that like crazy. My hair had only just recently recovered from those years of baldness. It was long for the first time in ages. "Well," he said, "I am going out for the day. I will talk to you about it when I get home tonight."

I went through everything that day. I knew very well he would be able to talk me into it that night. It must have been a very valuable experience or he would not have done it. Besides, every single assignment Leonard had ever given me was valuable. Of course he would talk me into it! "I might as well just choose it," I thought.

That night I said to Leonard, "You don't have to say another word. I will do it," I told him.

"Good" he said. He seemed very happy about it.

Meanwhile, for the next eight days I was in total resistance. It was awful. My ego was roaring. My spine was in knots.

Second Visit

By this time I was willing to have things easier. I found my way to the ashram on donkey. Phil and I had a great time. We arrived there in the late afternoon, near dusk. The group was already in the garden chanting with Baba. I wondered what it would be like to see him again, knowing at the same time that I had never really left. You can't leave Babaji and he never leaves you, no matter what form his existence takes.

I approached, seeing him in the distance. He was passing out *prasad* (food blessed by the guru). Suddenly he threw me a piece (from where he was to me seemed like a very long distance). And yet the *prasad* landed exactly in my mouth. That was my welcome . . . just like a *dog*! Yes, I was home.

The next day he avoided me completely, wouldn't even look at me. Of course I didn't blame him. My resistance was way up — it was about shaving my head. Phil was going to shave his, too. We were both into resistance. (Babaji was processing him on war karma. He had been in Viet Nam, front lines, and lots of other wars in past lives. He had been reading war novels ever since London. He had been glued to them.) Babaji would not look at me the whole day. I finally went off alone that night and rebirthed myself. Afterwards he asked me to come sit with him. I cried and cried and cried. He did not say a word. He just kept on rebirthing me. I began to really acknowledge him as the father of rebirthing, just as Leonard had.

The next day was New Year's Day. Baba came out on the ledge of the mountain every hour that morning, standing over the cave, blessing everyone and all nations. I knew this was the day I had to do it. It was to be my initiation. I wanted to surrender completely. I could not wait any longer. I chose it. I thought it was about time. I checked with him. He was coming down the path. I was a bit nervous as he approached. "Is it time for my *moodunn* (headshave) Baba?" As if I didn't know!

"Oh yes" he replied and smiled.

I started searching for the barber. He was a little tiny man who carried a box and wore a bell around his neck. So I was listening for the bell. It took no time at all to find him. We went down by the river. I had asked all the Americans to come and support me. They stood around in a circle with me in the middle, and chanted. Fortunately for me, there were *seven* LRT graduates there that year. They were such a solace to me. I was proud the way they were handling things. The were not getting sick like many others. I had prepared them well and they had prepared themselves well.

Baba was very good to them. I told them to get busy and help the other devotees who were having a harder time. Baba appreciated that.

The little barber opened the box. I was shocked. There was what looked like the most ancient razor I had ever seen. It looked literally hundreds of years old! He began chanting very loud, took over my mind. *Zip Zip*. He was moving very fast, very fast. I saw my long red hair floating down the Ganges! It was amazingly exciting. I started crying and crying. It was not because of the loss of hair this time. It was a complete opening. It was one of the most religious experiences of my life and it was over so fast! People were rubbing my head. Several decided to follow. I rubbed my head. It was an amazing feeling. I felt just like a newborn.

"Oh, I should start a new book on birth," was my next thought. "I should start it today." I was all finished with *The Only Diet There Is* except for the art work of the dedication page. (I usually did not start a new book until I was totally done with the previous.) I went to sit down on the bank, by myself, meditating on my head. Just then, an LRT grad from Washington, D.C. came to me. She had arrived that day. "Sondra, I have a present for you from Don Wyman. It is some artwork you asked him if he would do once." She handed me a folder. I was shocked. I had forgotten that I had asked Don if he would draw me some grape leaves. They were perfect. That had been the *only* thing left on that book and *there it was*, instant completion. Another miracle at Hherakhan. Well, I took that as a direct sign that I was to start a new book that very day.

I promised myself I would get major portions done before going to London even though I had never written a book in longhand before. I wondered what it would be like to write a book without a typewriter. I decided I better go meditate in the cave first. After all, I had finally earned the right! I had shaved my head.

I went to the cave. There was Prem Baba guarding the cave. He remembered me from the last visit and all the singing he did to me. He rubbed my head and bowed to me; and then he said, "Okay, you can go in."

Nobody had told me what it was like in there. There was a room you pass through which led to the most perfect cave in the back that I had ever seen (having been a "spelunker" at the University of Florida, I had seen a few caves in my day). Baba's presence was everywhere. It was like crawling into his very body. I immediately fell to the ground sobbing. I was into a rebirthing, like you would not believe. I sobbed, I breathed, and I shook. I was absolutely not used to that much energy. Prem Baba became my "rebirther." He would crawl in there just when I needed him and chant to me, rock me, rub my body with ashes and he would love me almost like nobody had ever loved me. He seemed to turn into Babaji. I had that same distinct feeling again. Then I would get it together and he would go back and sit out front as if I was not even there. I would stay in there two to three hours a day, every other day, trying to get clear on the book *(Ideal Birth)*. It was to be a very controversial book, being about underwater birth in the U.S.

I wrote on the book every day, two hours a day, for two weeks. During "karma yoga" I would always ask Baba if I could go sit under his tree and write instead of carry rocks. He would always let me, also knowing that I desperately needed a rest. He was extremely good to me that visit. He let me write and be at peace.

❧

That year, however, I was not assigned to a private room. He made us sleep on a warehouse floor with the peasants and the feedsacks. It was a new experience, to say the least. One day I decided to write letters to every single person on my staff, acknowledging them for their work that year. I spent hours on these letters. I stacked them up on the makeshift altar I had made out of an old crate. When I was finished, I remember thinking that there was one line in those letters that was "off." That wording was off — my ego again. I fell into a deep sleep. The candle was burning on my altar. I always woke up for evening temple — after all, who could sleep through those loud bells? Usually, I never could actually sleep during siesta time anyway. I never did need much sleep. But that day was different. I was in a stupor. All through siesta, all through the afternoon, and *even* throughout the bell ringing and temple, I slept. I awoke late, to some very loud screaming. It was a German devotee who had run out of the temple early to look for his "smoke." He saw my altar on fire. The top was burning up in huge flames, and he was trying to put it out. I was horrified. Baba had obviously put it in his head to leave the temple, *saving me*! The amazing part about it was that all the letters in the pile had burned up with that one wrong line in them. The three at the bottom of the pile *without* that line were not even scarred. Amazing but true. That was the beginning of my altar fires. I have had five in my life since, some *spontaneous* combustion (in the U.S.) when there were not candles lit at all!

After the fire I thought, "Well, I should have known I had it coming." Prior to that, this trip had been altogether too calm to believe. I continued writing, every day carrying my manuscript around in a black bag. I was pretty proud of what I had written. It was a combination of all my years as a prenatal nurse, and all my years as a rebirther rolled together.

The day before I was to leave, I noticed in *darshan* line that Babaji looked very intensely at my black bag with X-ray vision. I wondered why. It was an omen. That day in the cave I literally freaked out. A past-life memory came up for me of being pregnant and having a dead fetus I could not deliver. It was awful. I tried to rebirth myself through it, but I couldn't. The energy was too much, too weird. I came crawling out of the cave on my hands and knees, wondering where Prem Baba was. I grabbed the first devotee I saw (German) and asked him to take me up to my bunk and then asked him go to find Phil. "Phil, you must rebirth me. I am having a heavy past-life memory about pregnancy." He was wonderful. "I am not surprised," he said calmly. "You have been working on that book two straight weeks."

He did the best he could among the feedsacks and peasants. Then I suddenly remembered the manuscript. *Where was it?* My black bag was missing! I jumped up. I had to go find it. I ran across the river. It was nowhere. Not in the cave. Not anywhere. It was gone. I was so very upset. I took a long walk by myself along the Ganges, realizing that Babaji must have dematerialized it. "It must have been off base . . ." I thought. Then I talked in my mind to Baba. I told him he should keep it if it was off. I would go to London, lock myself up, and start all over. I was letting go, but then the last thing I did on that walk was yell out, "But if it *is* right, I want it back."

That night in *darshan* I was very embarrassed. I wanted to talk to Baba about it. I kneeled down ashamed. "Baba," I said, "I have lost my manuscript."

It was the only time he ever reprimanded me verbally. Even so, he was soft: "Why are you so careless?" he asked.

"I have no excuse," I replied.

"Well," he said, taking pity on me again, "I'll put out a search warrant on it" (as if he didn't know were it was!).

The next day, Monte, an ex-lawyer from Seattle, LRT grad, came up to me and said, "I think I know where it could be."

"You are kidding. We have looked everywhere."

"Did you check the priest's quarters?"

"I don't even know where that is, Monte."

"Come with me."

He led me across the river again, above the cave to a secret little room where all the holiest objects were stored. There it was. The black bag, perfectly safe with all the holiest objects of the ashram!

I was so happy. But that was not the first nor the last time Baba disappeared the manuscript and reappeared it. It took me over a year to understand what he was doing.

Just in time, I got it back. I ran to say goodbye to Baba and thank him.

The last thing he said was, "Take your camera, take your camera, take your camera, take your camera."

My camera was right there in the side pocket of my back pack. I *was* taking it. Why was he telling me to take it when I was taking it? Why was he repeating the same sentence over and over and over?

Sometimes I did not understand him at all.

The next night in New Delhi somewhat in our room stole my camera while I was asleep. It took me a long time to understand that.

Back in the U.S.

I recovered from India a lot faster this time — I was in a lot better shape. Less ego. I worked on the manuscript some more in the following months; but then a funny thing happened. It disappeared again. In fact, *all* copies dematerialized, even the one in safe-keeping, and even the one the publishers had. This seemed incredible. Three manuscripts disappearing? This had never happened at my publishers before. This was to happen one more time before it was all over. Later, much later, I came to realize that Baba was protecting me. That manuscript was too controversial. It would have stirred up too much resistance in the medical profession. The time was not right. One thing for sure, Baba is an expert on timing. The other miracle was that later I got to finish it at the right place — New Zealand, where much underwater birth research had been done.

As for the camera incident, he wanted to get my attention on cameras, because one of these days I was going to have to be a public figure and be photographed a lot. I had had a very embarrassing incident as a child around cameras that needed to be cleared. It came up after my camera was stolen. I still am healing my relationship to cameras.

So then we went back to the States, heads shaved. I wondered what my mother would think. We were to leave our heads shaved for nine months, the period of the womb. This was a special purification. I wondered what it would be like teaching. I could always wear a turban, of course. But I wanted to learn to be comfortable in public either way.

My first night back in the U.S. one of my friends decided I should be treated to a movie. Seemed like a good enough idea. But the movie happened to be "*Altered States!*" I was *already* in an altered state, and we were in Los Angeles, mind you. It was freaky. During the middle of the movie, when the scientists were coming out of the Lilly-Tanks on drugs and turned into animals, I did freak out. I temporarily went right out of my body. And then, I heard the *Voice* again. It was Baba. He said: "You must do the God Training. It is not a question of *will* you do it, or *can* you do it. This must be done."

I came crashing in my body saying, "Okay." But then I wondered what on earth I had committed to. What *was* the

God Training? This haunted me for over a year. It wasn't until I finally went away to Bali in solitude that I got what is should be.

Those nine months with my head shaved were really something. I was prepared not to be with any man, quite sure that no man would look at me. I found the opposite to be true. Men were fascinated with it — with me — and I had more advances than usual. I went about freely with no scarf or turban until I learned to be comfortable. Sometimes when I worked, I would wear a scarf, depending on my best judgment. My mother cried, but then she got over it when I told her that I was sure she would not deny me the most religious experience of my life.

At the end of nine months it was time to complete the process. My hair was about an inch long. I remember the ninth month arriving. I said, "Oh, I can grow out my hair now." But that night a strange thing happened. I suddenly had this very intense, almost sexual desire to shave my head again, to the scalp with a blade. I had been shaving it with an electric razor so there had always been some fuzz instead of the shiny scalp. I could not believe how strong the desire was. I was in New York City. I closed my door and sat down before my altar and looked at Baba's picture for hours and hours. Was I not complete on this? Did he want me to do it all over? It was 3 A.M. I received a sudden phone call from a man I was dating in Washington, D.C. He was calling me from a phone booth, strange hour I thought. We were chatting and he suddenly said, "*Wow*, I would not see this scene in twenty years! A monk just got out of his car with his head shaved . . ." Well, that was it. I hung up the phone and knew I had to do it again. Doing it to the scalp with a blade is one thing in India, but in New York City it is another. Fortunately, Fredric was in town. His years practicing Tai Chi made me certain it would be fine. We held the ceremony at David Lambert's loft. David sang the Lord's prayer. Fred did it carefully. It took a very long time. It made us very close. For some reason he had to do that, we had to go through that together.

Life went on. I worked harder than ever that year. But I kept being haunted by the commitment I had made about the God Training.

During the time between my visits to the ashram, I would take advantage of the fact that the guru is one's mother, father, lover, husband, wife, confidant, psychiatrist, and best friend. I wanted someone to bear my soul to, and I know that that was one function of the guru. I would be foolish not to use him that way. I wrote him hundreds of letters bearing my soul, since my way of clearing myself is writing — and he knew that. It didn't matter to me if he read the letters. Writing them healed me. I was told later that he always passed his hand over my letters and that he knew everything in them. Of course, I didn't really need to even write them for him to get what I was thinking. The guru knows your whole mind, your whole soul, your whole life past, present, and future. You have to be willing to be completely exposed. However, I continued writing to him anyway as therapy for myself. I would send him pretty cards, often taking a long time to pick them out just in case he did see them. Of course he could "see" right through the envelope obviously since he was able to "see" what was going on in any country at any given time just by a wave of his hand . . . a scene would appear on the wall of his room. He could check out New York, for example, at any time and get full scenes.

So I sent pretty cards. His secretary told me once that he took to opening my cards and tearing off the pictures and would give the pictures to the local peasants telling them to decorate their walls with this "art." It made me laugh to think of my cards pasted upon on the walls of the local peasants in the huts along the Ganges. Other reported they would see my notes floating down the river at times. My words were going everywhere. But those were not often my highest thoughts. Those were often some of my stressful thoughts that I would lay at his feet. The Ganges purified them. They would disappear for me that way. And Baba always answered my questions, usually immediately, or within two days, long before the letter could have ever gotten near India in actuality. He would answer as soon as I could receive the answer. Sometimes he would answer by actually dictating a letter to me.

I had no plans to return to India. I just wanted to get clear on the God Training I had committed to. I had to get away, figure out what it was, meditate, write. It seemed that everybody wanted me to come to their city. I had trouble saying no. I was never going to get this God Training going unless I went far away, very far away. Going to Bali seemed right. I had always dreamed of going to Bali, the island of the Gods.

❧

It had to be the perfect place to write the God Training. But I didn't even know where Bali was! Finally at the Rebirthing Jubilee in Colorado, I just went down to the travel agent and bought a ticket. Indonesia? How do you get there? Fourteen thousand islands in Indonesia! Bali was just one of fourteen thousand islands.

It took days and days on the plane. I was in a daze. I knew no one there and nothing about it. Fortunately, I saw an ad for the Oberoi Hotel, so I went there the first night. Thank you again Biki Oberoi. But obviously I could not afford staying there for months, and I might be in Bali months. Who knows? My first morning in Bali I had breakfast by the ocean. The people were so sweet that I cried. Dear God, what has happened to the Western World?

Thanks to a wonderful Balinese man named "Big William," who became my guide and support system, the next day I found my way to Poppie's Cottages in Kuta Beach, and for the next six weeks I was in solitude and bliss in Bali. I could write a whole book on that experience alone. Bali taught me a lot. Bali was perfect for what I had to do. Bali is in my heart forever. Oh, Bali, where every single family has a temple and they use the temple daily without fail. People were like Saints. People bowed to me. I was in Heaven.

One day after I had been there for weeks working on the God Training and feeling immense joy and satisfaction, Babaji appeared to me. He was wearing bright red. He motioned to me, calling me to India.

As I said, this was not in my plans, I had not considered it. But here it was. I even received a telegram from him stating that instead of going up to the ashram I should meet him in Delhi and go on tour with him. What a chance — to go on tour with Babaji? I started getting packed immediately. Funny how he could send telegrams when I told no one my address!

I had to go to Singapore to get my visa.

In the New Delhi airport, all the luggage from all flights was piled in one big pile. Things were a mess. Somebody was trying to bribe his way into the country. My line was held up for an hour. I was resisting India again. But once I was out of the airport and on my way to the Angeli House I was so happy. I walked in to the beautiful music of the sitar. And then I had a very big surprise. Babaji had sent Leonard down the mountain a day early to greet me. Leonard had been up in the ashram for the six weeks I was in Bali. I did not know he was still in India, and he did not know I was coming. The timing was amazing. I walked in and he walked in right after me — one of the little surprises of Baba. Leonard was so happy to see me he jumped right up in the air. "Well, Len," I said, "How perfect . . . let's go to the movie *Ghandi* tonight." Baba was coming down the next day. It was very powerful to see that movie, just released, in India. Furthermore, we sat there, both feeling Baba come toward us. It was very heavy. The movie affected me a lot — or was it Baba's arrival? I told Len I had to go home. I couldn't even talk to him. In my room that night I trembled for hours. I was obviously having some more purification. The next morning I met Leonard for breakfast in a nice hotel. He stunned me with his acknowledgement. (He never acknowledged me much. I didn't need it and it didn't matter. We had too much to do.)

"I've been meditating on you all night, Sondra."

"Really?" I inquired. "What about?"

"Your superconscious is way ahead of your subconscious."

"Is that a problem, Leonard?" I wanted to know, not sure what he meant.

"I mean, it does not matter what you say anymore, your presence will heal everyone." That day I was complete with him as my teacher.

I was pretty speechless.

When Baba came, things happened very fast. We followed him to Bombay. Leonard and I were allowed to stay in the home of some very wealthy devotees on the beach. We had five servants. What a switch from the usual ashram life! We would get up at 3 A.M. every morning, the driver would drive us for one hour across Bombay, and at 4 A.M. we would be standing in line for *darshan*. Thousands were there. How different it was from the ashram life, the small groups we were used to. The devotees were very lavish in Bombay. They had been sewing silks for Baba all year. They would give him a new set of clothes every single hour!

After *darshan* we would go sit in a huge tent. Then we would chant. Then we would wait in another line for hours to kneel before him. In the afternoon we would line up in a different line, going up and down the steps to where he was on the top floor. In the evening we would chant and stand in more lines. We would be with him like that from 4 A.M. until 11 P.M.

It was amazing to see how he handled the thousands. He never got tired. He would laugh the whole time. One day he called me up front to sit with him and kept throwing flowers on my head and singing, "Sondra Ray, Sondra Ray," as if it were a mantra. I should have known he was building me up for some big thing. He definitely was getting me ready for something.

It was very exciting to be on tour with Babaji as he visited many different homes of his devotees. They would spend months and months waiting and preparing for his arrival, and when he came, there would be tremendous celebration and love. In the home where I was staying a feast was prepared, even though Babaji ate almost nothing. We decorated the living room for many days in advance. My job was to pin fresh roses on all the curtains. I loved to watch the host prepare the altar. We spent many hours singing *bajans*, waiting for his arrival. The home was purified by this and took on a rosy glow. When Babaji would arrive, it was always very exciting. Everyone would get very stirred up. Many people would come for *darshan*. He would go from home to home all day, never getting tired. Sometimes he would laugh and laugh and throw water on everyone, kind of like a baptism.

❧

One day he surprised us by suddenly shouting out to the crowds, in English, "rebirthing is 'in' and I'm in the mood for it!"

There were very few of us Americans there. It was clear that the Indians did not know what he was talking about. Then he called me up front and instructed me to go rebirth this famous Indian movie star, an Orson Wells-Richard Burton type. I was driven to his home. Fortunately, the man spoke English. It was a very very difficult rebirthing. The man was a chain smoker and borderline alcoholic. I knew of Baba's intense love for this devotee. On the way back to the ashram, I said to Baba in my mind, "Why don't you just heal this guy totally of his smoking habit and drinking habit all at once? I know you could do it . . ."

Baba gave me the answer like a flash. I had been dealing with some low grade symptoms. He suddenly "disappeared them" all at once. The light that hit my body was so shocking I nearly fainted. As it was, I fell to the ground. "See," he said, "You could barely handle that. This man is not ready for that much light. That is why I sent you there. He needs a little at a time."

After a couple weeks of this intense regime, he sent Leonard off to China. He called me up front, saying, "You come with me to Vapi." I had no idea where Vapi was. It turned out to be a small dusty cow town that he had adopted. The night before I went off with him, I noticed I was the only Anglo-Saxon in the tent with thousands of Indians. He had sent all the Americans home, or on ahead, and the Europeans, too. It was a very strange feeling for me. When it was my turn up in *darshan* line, and I knelt before him, he wrapped me swiftly in very powerful white light. I wondered what on earth he was preparing me for.

Once we got to the little town of Vapi, we were located in a kind of farm house of some devotees. I was very relieved to see an American there named Mark from California and a few German devotees. Altogether, there were only about fifteen of us, even counting the Indians. This is what I had waited for forever. The intimacy of being with him, in a living room, no less.

I was ordered to sleep on the kitchen floor. Now *that* was a switch after the mansion and five servants! I had slept on a lot of floors before, but never on a kitchen floor. It was obvious what he was doing. I was born in the kitchen (nobody else had to sleep on the kitchen floor). He was obviously processing more of my birth trauma. Now, kitchen floors in India are not what you imagine a kitchen floor in the states. I woke up with a splitting headache — what I would imagine a migraine to be like. I never got headaches, let alone migraines. Besides, someone had stolen my American shoes.

We were told to meet Baba early in the morning in the living room for *darshan*. There was a swing placed in the living room decorated with many flowers. He was in a very good mood, laughing and laughing, swinging higher and higher like a kid. The moment I was waiting for was ruined by the intensity of my head pain. I could not bear to look at him for one second. The pain was too great. I could not stand it. For the first time in my life I wanted to leave him and leave India forever — and I was serious. I prayed for a miracle. In my mind I said to him telepathically, "Either I get a miracle right now or I have to leave permanently."

In no time at all, a tray was passed out with some silver glasses on it. He said it was "medicine" and stated that there were a few of us who needed this, looking right at me, of course. I drank some. I had no idea what it was . . . seemed like herbs. Baba got up and left.

It was then that I realized that I had forgotten to change some traveller's checks into rupees in Bombay. I had no Indian money. I thought I better go downtown to a bank and change some money. It seemed like a small town, so I went alone. The streets were bustling with very dark Indians, many cows, bikes, horses, rickshaws, and other animals, Nobody seemed to speak English. I finally found a bank. They refused, hardly being able to understand me, and saying, "This is not Bombay." I went back outside, suddenly feeling very poor, like an Indian. I had no good shoes and only 4.30 in rupees. I got very paranoid. I still had a severe headache, and I felt sick. I grabbed a rickshaw and demanded that the driver find me a bank where I could change traveller's checks. He started going to the edge of town. I suddenly began to feel like a very rich American compared to these people. I had everything compared to them. Who did I think I was? I felt very rich one minute, very poor the next, and very sick the next. Something was happening to me. I felt strange. My headache started to loosen up. I burst into tears. Oh, the medicine was working at last.

All of a sudden I realized we were out in the country. Where on earth had this driver taken me? He dropped me off and pointed to a bank. It was closed. Why was this bank in the country and why was it closed and why was he leaving me here?

"You wait here until it opens," he said.

I wondered why it had different hours than other banks. I didn't know where I was, and I had forgotten to write down the directions of the farm house. I sat on the ground and cried. A sweet little Indian man told me to go sit inside the bank and wait until it opened. Why was the door open? There was absolutely nobody in there. Not any tellers, not any guards, not any janitors, even. I sat there by myself feeling very strange. All of a sudden it occurred to me that I had taken something besides just herbs. It "came on" strong (later I found out it was "Bong" — dentura plant). I started feeling Babaji enter my body, pushing something out. I was very scared. I said, "Take it easy on me." Then I said, "No, sock it to me."

I would flash back and forth, breathing like mad. I breathed and breathed and breathed, rebirthing myself as much as possible, feeling like I was dying. All of a sudden it came up. The past life. Somebody was killing me in a bank. I had died in a bank. No wonder I was always terrified in banks and terrified around numbers and bookkeeping.

I remember saying, "Oh, I am dying right here in India and nobody even knows where I am . . ." I was fading out. I finally went through it. I died.

And then suddenly the lights went on! The bank was opening! There were tellers coming in, janitors, people bustling about.

I could not believe my eyes. I was alive. And there were two German devotees standing right in front of me. How did they find this bank? "Do you need help, Sondra?" they were asking.

"Help? Well, yes, I can hardly move . . . could you get this traveller's check cashed?"

They did. No problem.

Was I in a dream?

They took me back to the farm house in a nice taxi. I could not move. I was sick as a dog with diarrhea. My roommate Motu was really wonderful. She had no problem handling me.

The next day we were herded into a large truck. Baba was having a celebration for the whole town. He fed the whole town. There was food for two thousand people, but three thousand came. Somehow more food was suddenly there. The director told me he does not know how it happened that they could feed an extra thousand. I was sick as a dog, lying on the ground the whole time.

The very next morning it was time for me to leave. I had to catch a train back to Bombay in order for me to make my international flight. I received word that Babaji had assigned me an escort. He turned out to be a very handsome Indian movie star! (I will never get over that one.) At 4 A.M. we got up for the fire ceremony. It was the last time I ever saw Babaji in that body.

He was feeding the fire, an ancient ceremony done for thousands of years. He suddenly looked up at me with that piercing look. Then he said to me, telepathically, "You *finally* got through it." I burst into tears. The tears shot out of my eyes toward him in a straight horizontal line without falling to the ground.

I knew he had healed my money case, probably saved me decades and decades of time on my money karma; maybe hundreds of years. It had been worth it.

That night my wealthy hosts in Bombay threw me a big farewell party with many Indian delicacies. I was feeling fine, very healthy.

April 1991
Mayan Temple of Inscriptions
Palenque, Mexico

The following information I had already written a few times earlier between 1984 and 1990; however the papers always mysteriously "disappeared". I decided I would try it one more time at this sacred spot. I told Babaji that if the papers disappeared again, I would therefore assume that it was not meant to be published.

I climbed up to the top of this ancient Mayan temple overlooking the ruins and wrote the following in long hand. I felt that the energy of Palenque might ground me enough that I could hang onto it this time.

February 1984
Babaji's Samadhi

It was the break of an LRT in L.A. on Sunday. The group was a bit tough; so I was wet rebirthing myself in my hotel room bathtub. I was saying to Babaji that I was willing to get totally aligned with him. I suddenly was given the message to hold my first public chanting on Monday night after the training. Oddly enough, a student's brother had had a dream that I came to their home and brought eighty people. She had just told me this dream which had made no sense to me until now. So I got out of the water and called her and said, "Remember the dream your brother had? Well, how about tomorrow night? I need a place to hold a chanting." She said, "Fine."

After the break, I announced it to the training body. I had no idea how many would actually come, as it was definitely optional; and many had to leave town Monday morning. Interestingly enough, exactly eighty did show up. I had told no one about the dream.

The large home we went to was absolutely perfect. It was like a temple. The living room had thick white carpets with large brass candlesticks which were lit when we came in. I could hardly believe that the living room was big enough to hold everyone very nicely. It was a huge place. On top of that, it was built by a famous man, her grandfather, who had written music for a extremely successful Broadway musical. I had been a bit nervous about chanting in public for the first time. I had only done it in private. I carefully explained the meaning and the power of chanting the mantra *Om Namaha Shivaya*, and then I just started doing it. Soon everyone was chanting with me, and two hours flew by. We were surprised right after that to hear shouting from outside the house, yelling for us to come out immediately. Two students who had left early had looked up in the sky and seen a very unusual phenomenon. There was a huge blue cross in the sky over the house and L.A. All of us saw it. We were all stunned. None of us had ever seen anything like it and we had no idea what it meant.

Now today, I understand that that was when Babaji took Samadhi, merging his electrons with the universe. (Apparently his last words were: "I am going to explode my heart and give a piece to everyone." This he did consciously on February 14. (I calculated the time difference later, and it all made sense).

I went on to Tucson, not understanding the meaning of the cross, because I had no idea of Baba's plans. In Tucson, a devotee called me from L.A., saying that Babaji had "died." She was crying and was very upset. I was remarkably calm and not upset at all. I knew he knew exactly what he was doing; and that there was a reason for his departure and I knew it had to be "conscious." I told her I would change my route to Toronto, and stop over in L.A. again and calm everyone down. I suddenly "understood" what had happened when we saw the cross. So off I went, back to L.A.

Rhonda and Mannie, (the L.A. Center Managers for the LRT), picked me up at the airport. We drove out of the airport and suddenly I said, "Stop the car right here. I need to make a call and find out what is the appropriate public statement." I did not know why I could not wait until we got to the house, but it seemed urgent. We went into a near airport hotel. I turned *left*. Rhonda said, "No, no, the phones are over here," pointing to the right. But I kept turning left. Immediately I ran right into Michael Jackson, who had just been burned by the Pepsi Cola Ad. I had never met him before. It was sad to see him looking like a wounded bird. He was with his bodyguard, who looked like a wrestler. It was strange, but somehow they both looked like angels. I thought I saw their "higher selves." I did not say anything, I just sent them a lot of energy and love. Then I went to the phones. After my call, Mannie came and said, "Sondra, he is still out there in the car." I said "Okay, then take him my card." Mannie went out, knocked on the window, and Michael rolled it down with his white gloved hand. Mannie said, "Here, call Sondra, she will help you." Then they drove off. I did not understand the meaning of all this, but it seemed very auspicious to meet him at that moment. By the phone was a big metal brass piece that said, "Emergency Departures." I wondered why did Baba take a departure *now*; and why did I run into Michael Jackson now?

In Toronto, I was a house guest of a female Rolfer and her son. It was still only a few days into the first week after Babaji's Samadhi. Babaji began appearing to me in startling ways at night. He showed me he was forever alive and there. Now I try to imagine what it must have been like to have me as a house guest that week. I acknowledge them for the way they handled it!

Vision: First Night.

I was attending a huge funeral . . . like that of the Pope. I had to stand in a very long line facing the casket . . . there were so many people that it seemed like I was in line for days. When I finally got to the front of the line and looked in the casket, I recognized the corpse. It was Babaji. But he had a different body; it was definitely the same head, however. (Once he had appeared to me, floating in the air with a baby's body and an old man's head from a different materialization . . . so I was not too surprised. I merely said, "Oh, its Babaji!")

Suddenly the corpse became alive and he opened his eyes and looked at me, giving me the most love I have ever experienced in my life in one exchange. I was completely overwhelmed and felt like I could not handle much more. Suddenly people began pushing me aside. As I was shoved away, Babaji raised his arm from the casket, waving goodbye to me. The amazing thing was that he raised his arm in the exact way, with the exact same speed, that my father had done from his hospital bed before he drifted into his final coma. What struck me was how Babaji was processing me also at the same time on my Dad's death; while giving me the most incredible *darshan*. Suddenly I was at a party saying to people, "They are having trouble keeping that man dead back there."

Teleportation: Second Night.

Suddenly I was teleported to India. I was walking down the streets and it was totally real, not like a dream at all. The sounds, the smells, etc. were all real. Not one thing was distorted. I knew I was really there. I began hearing Babaji say things into my ear. It was a major teaching I was getting; and I felt it was too fast to integrate. So I decided to go to my hotel room. I needed to concentrate. My hotel room was on the top floor of the hotel. I lay down on the bed and looked out the window for a minute. Suddenly I saw a beautiful woman walking by. She was so incredibly beautiful that I exclaimed, "This is the most beautiful woman I have seen in all lifetimes!" But then I suddenly began shouting, "Wait a minute, there are no sidewalks up here!" I ran to the window to look out and I saw that she was walking on air!

Then suddenly I came crashing back into my body in Toronto. I was in shock. (Later I realized it was Babaji appearing to me in the form of the Divine Mother.)

Vision: Third Night.

There was a casket in my bedroom and it was open! Inside was a corpse; and it seemed to have been dead for ages. There was only a skeleton really and its bones were very brittle and loaded with cobwebs.

As I began to peer into the casket, the situation changed completely. The corpse-skeleton began to regenerate itself! First it began to grow muscles and fascia and so on. I was in a kind of trance over this; but I was not afraid. Then it began to grow skin. Finally it sat up and faced me and began to crawl out of the casket. Then it stood up and faced me. I was in awe. It began walking toward me, growing more and more alive as it walked toward me. It became more and more alive and more and more whole.

Suddenly a woman standing next to me began screaming: "Sondra, you are into some very heavy stuff . . . resurrecting the dead!" Then she fainted. (End of vision.)

It was years before I could bring myself to ask about that. I waited until the right moment when I could get Shastriji the high Priest, alone, with a translator whom I could trust. Then I asked him the meaning. He said that "because of my past lives, I was allowed to see Babaji's resurrected body. And that was *real*." "The woman who fainted," he said, "represented the Maya."

The Fourth, Sixth, and Seventh Nights

For three nights I had the following experiences:

I would automatically begin hyperventilating so intensely that my only thought was, "If I don't surrender completely right now, I will be in total body paralysis. There is no other alternative. I choose to surrender." Babaji seemed to be inside my body rebirthing me.

Very loud sounds would come out of me that were impossible to control. The sounds were startling even to me. They seemed to be like the sound of old lions roaring from ancient caves.

The following mornings I would get up and go down to the kitchen and find the woman and her son quite frightened. They told me that they heard the sounds and they were very afraid something was wrong with me. But when they would try to get up to help me, they each separately experienced being unable to move. They were "frozen" in their beds. I tried to tell them I was fine and that I was having some kind of exorcism.

I think they were probably very relieved when I left . . .

An Unusual Speech in Florida

I felt completely "fried" after that week; and could hardly stand up. And yet, I had to make it to a seminar in Florida. I was told there were over one hundred people already signed up. When Mikela met me at the airport, I told her to get me to the best chiropractor as fast as possible. He did not know me at all. But when he came in the room, he was very startled to see me . . . and he blurted out: "*What* have you been *doing*?" Then I blurted out: "Leaving my body at night, going to India and, well, I cannot explain it all right now." I told him about the seminar the next day. He worked on me about an hour and got me standing up straight.

The next day I had no idea what I was saying. I had to have continuing body work at every break. The only thing I remember is that I got the best record of enrollments for the coming LRT that I had ever gotten in my life. People would get up while I was talking and go back to the enrollment table and sign right up. I must have been in an alterted state. I did not tell them what had happened the previous week. I was not ready to talk about it.

Fire Purification

For the next two weeks, my bones felt like they were on fire. It was unusual enough to feel one's bones. On top of that, there seemed to be a real fire going on inside them. I did understand this to be some kind of purification from my guru, so I was not upset; except it was *very* intense; and I was preparing to go on my first world tour alone.

Beginning a World Tour in A Shocking Manner

It began in Alaska. I had an appointment with the press, so I got up early to meditate. I was sitting up, completely awake. Suddenly Babaji came to me, totally alive and in the flesh. I was not asleep, and it was not a vision. He took me into an "empty room." He had me stand next to him on one side of the room. Then he instructed me to begin walking with him, step by step with him in perfect alignment. (I remembered that I had told him I was willing to be perfectly aligned with him. Now here it was.) We walked across the room like that and then back to where we had started. Then he shocked me by picking me up in his arms and holding me like a baby. And he rocked me in his arms. He was definitely *not* dead and I was definitely *not* asleep. Of that I was certain. It was the most *real* experience I had ever had; but I could not explain it. Suddenly I was there meditating on the bed and someone was coming in the room. She was shocked at my appearance. She said, "You are glowing like an angel . . . and your hair has grown quite a lot! What is happening?"

My first world tour alone went like a breeze. I worked extremely hard and visited many countries. I never once got sick or even tired. Nor was I checked at any border. My last stop before returning to America was Melbourne, Australia. The night all my work was done, I was relaxing on the floor with a man who suddenly began acting very strangely. He seemed to "change" and began bowing to me continuously.

Later he told me that Babaji had possessed his body and was acknowledging me.

1984 to 1989

Since that week in 1984, I have not seen Babaji as often . . . approximately once a year perhaps. However, my relationship has deepened as I have opened more. The appearances I have had usually came after I have completed writing projects.

Most of these were at night, but I cannot really call them dreams because Babaji told us that it is impossible to make up a dream about him. When you see him at night, he actually came. I am not able to explain how this works.

After writing *Pure Joy* in Australia, he was suddenly "there" instructing me to sit next to him on his *asan*. Then he materialized a ball of fire in his left hand and placed it on the ground at our feet.

After finishing the book on physical immortality (*How to Be Chic, Fabulous and Live Forever*) in Hawaii, he appeared in miniature form only a few inches tall at my feet. He was totally complete and alive; but he was "pocket size."

On one July 4, when I was in Philadelphia, he appeared and showed me the future . . . precisely a certain event that I will participate in. He was preparing me.

After finishing a recent manuscript about my life (called *There's a Cow In My Bathtub*) he appeared as a King dressed in clothes made out of jewels. The jewels were also "alive," and I saw them "breathing." He told me to come with him for a ride in a chariot. We went down a secret road, and there was a palace also made out of the "breathing jewels." It was alive, and I was amazed that it could change size.

Sometimes when I have been too blocked he will appear to a clairvoyant in the vicinity and that person will call me to relate the messages. Usually they are stunned by this and their lives begin to change drastically after that.

1990

During this year, in India, I had a vision that I was on top of a very narrow mountain that was very hard to climb, and it was so thin that only two people could stand on the top. It was very hard to make it up there, and when I got to the top, there was Shastriji, Babaji's high priest. He began doing ceremonies with me, and we did a special *Aarti*. Later, when I told Shastriji about this, he told me that this was a turning point, and that I would now go through rapid spiritual changes. I could not imagine what that would be. I felt like I had been through so much already that I kind of wanted a break.

When I came back to the States, I began having very strange "episodes." For example, when my book *Inner Communion* came out, I had an intense reaction. My body felt like glass was shattering all through it. I could hardly stand up. My spiritual advisors told me that the old structure was breaking down. I went through temporary periods of old age, including something like rheumatism. I felt so strange; it was something like bad drug trips I've heard about. I would get paranoid. I would cry for hours on the floor before my altar. Sometimes I would wonder if I could make it. But there was always a miracle: a healer would come in my life that knew what to do: a body worker or a clairvoyant who would somehow understand. They would explain to me that my electromagnetic fields were being worked on; and that I was receiving "transcendent energy" from another dimension. It was scary at times. The end of 1990 and the beginning of 1991 were extremely difficult on my body. But, fortunately, I did not get sick, probably because I stuck it out with my spiritual practices.

I wondered: Was *this* what I had agreed to? Was this part of what I had asked for? I was told that the leaders had to go through this; and I was not the only one feeling these things.

What saved me was the certainty that by the grace of my guru, I was being transformed to something new and going to a new level. Somehow I knew that Babaji was turning my life into something supremely divine. It was a mystery . . . all a mystery. But I knew that on the other side of all these changes was ecstasy.

The Divine Mother

ༀ

Happy resident of Haidakhan,
you capture the minds of the whole world
Merciful Great Goddess
Hail to Thee, O Universal Mother, Consort of Shiva

When my guru took Samadhi (conscious departure), he said, "I am going to leave everything in the hands of the Divine Mother." I wondered what that meant, especially since he was not born of an earthly mother. Apparently he did, in fact, come from a divine mother when he materialized his body; but I did not really understand it.

My own mother is divine. I mean, she was really the perfect mother for me and still is. She certainly deserves acknowledgement as one of my most important teachers. The way she raised me was perfect for me. For one thing, I never felt "over parented." She let me be myself and just gave me a lot of "space." I could express myself freely and roam around. She always trusted me, and I felt that. Because I had her unconditional trust, I lived up to that and really did not give her a lot of trouble by getting into trouble. I was reliable and trustworthy. I can't say if I was that way because she treated me that way; or if she treated me that way because I was that way. Probably some of both.

I never really heard my mother complain, even though the most important man in her life (my dad) was sick and dying. I once asked her how she was able to cope and she said, "Well, Sondra . . . I had you girls . . . some women cannot even have children." She was always seeing the highest thought in every situation. I did not really appreciate that when I was growing up, because I thought all mothers must be like that. I have been surprised, over and over again, to find out that that is not the case, and that my mother was quite rare in her qualities. My mother made sure that there were no arguments in my presence. She said the Bible said to never let the sun set on your anger. I never saw her and Dad fighting, which is something for which I am extremely grateful. I never learned the habit of fighting — and I am glad of it.

My mother had a career and taught me the importance of being independent. She never complained about that either, although she was the only woman in our little town that worked. I thought she had to work because my dad was sick, but now I know she would have anyway. She was into making a contribution.

❧

In our Protestant church, we did not acknowledge the feminine aspect of God at all, so I never ever heard the term "The Divine Mother" until I went to India. And when Babaji made the statement of leaving *everything* in the hands of the Divine Mother, I thought I better find out the meaning. On the first anniversary of his *Samadhi*, I travelled to the very tip of India to visit the most ancient temple of the Divine Mother that I could find. I arrived late at night and was told that the *darshan* would be at 4:30 A.M. When I arose, I was surprised to learn that the temple was underground. What happened "down there" changed my life a great deal, and I would have to say it was one of those very real peak experiences.

This temple was around five thousand years old and the amazing thing is that the following scene I am going to describe has been going on *every single day* for five thousand years without fail! So try to imagine the power of *that*. The *murti* (statue with the living presence) was at the end of a tunnel, behind curtains. When they opened the curtains, we had to lean over a railing and look down the tunnel to see the ceremony. There were two priests, one on each side of the *murti*, which was dressed just like a woman, in beautiful clothes. With these clothes on, "she" actually looked very real . . . and alive.

The priests began by undressing her and getting her ready for her "bath." First, they scrubbed down her body carefully with sand using a toothbrush. Then they rinsed her off. They scrubbed every nook and cranny very carefully and this took a long time. After that rinsing, they began again, using a sandal-wood paste and toothbrush, doing it all over again in every nook and cranny. Then they rinsed her off again. Then they did a *third* scrubbing, with some other cleanser I did not recognize, that was even finer. Then they rinsed her *again*. She was sparkling by this time. Then, for the final thing, they took a silver pitcher of fresh milk and crushed many rose petals into the milk. Then they poured this rose milk over her head. As the rose milk ran down over her breasts, they caught it in another silver urn . . . singing chants all through this whole procedure. This milk "from her breasts" they then passed around for us to drink. Most people cried after that. I certainly did. I felt like the whole place filled up with a kind of rebirthing energy. I definitely felt rebirthed. It was just exquisite.

It was after that that I had the supreme privilege of meeting a four hundred-year-old woman. I had heard that she was sort of "guarding that town or that temple." Her age had been apparently checked out by one Indian master I respected. Anyway, I did not doubt it, and that is probably the reason I was allowed to meet her. I did not need to see it for proof either, as I had been studying physical immortality for several

years before that; and I had read about masters who were like
that. We found her sitting on the ground down a hidden alley-
like street. She was actually surrounded by twelve dogs. These
did not seem like ordinary dogs to me — they all seemed alike,
for one thing. I remember now thinking that they not only
looked alike, but they also had a strange kind of human quality.
We seemed to imagine them being her "devotees" in another
life. It was very unusual. I was not afraid of these dogs. She was
apparently welcoming us, and so I knew the dogs knew this
was okay.

The woman was in silence and had been so for many years.
I remember that she looked rather "transparent" . . . kind of
like tissue paper, but really alive. I obviously was a bit spaced
out, and find it all quite difficult to describe. I did not know
what to say or do at first, but then I remembered that I had
some *vibuti* (sacred ash) that was materialized by Saibaba. In
fact, it was really fresh, coming straight from the "Divine" only
a couple of days before. I gave it to her. She surprised me by
carefully putting some of it on the third eye of each dog, which
was something to observe. Then she put some on my third
eye. I felt like I had really had a *darshan* by the Divine Mother
now. It was my last experience in India on that trip. The next
day I left for Sri Lanka, satisfied beyond my wildest dreams.

¿₹

So that year I really began thinking about the Divine Mother a
lot. I was so happy to be tuned into the "feminine aspect of
God," that I decided to bring it into my home as much as
possible.

The next thing I did was commission a large painting of the
Divine Mother. I located Babaji's temple painter and asked her
to do it. She was out in the woods outside of Seattle at the time.
She went into a cabin along a lake and stayed in there a long
time, painting the painting. In fact, she stayed in there so many

months that I became afraid. "What if I don't like it after all that?" I said to a friend. I asked him to go out and see it. After all, he is an art critic. He stayed in there many hours and came out and said to me, "Sondra, it is very hypnotic." What a relief! If he liked it, it was going to be okay.

When it was finally delivered to me, I could not handle it at all. I felt it was just too much and it would dominate my whole house. It was so overpowering that I felt it should be put in an ashram. My decorator agreed, so we put it in storage. I went on tour as usual. However, one night he had a dream that he was supposed to hang it. So he got up, went to my apartment and did just that. I came home from my tour and when I opened my door . . . there *it* was. At first I was shocked, but then I suddenly said out loud to my empty room, "Well, okay . . . I will surrender."

It felt a little funny to be talking out loud when there was nobody there; but on the other hand, I was speaking to her and she actually "answered." Suddenly the room was filled with the perfume of roses. It was very strong and lasted quite a long time. It was not there when I had entered. It only came after I said I would surrender. After that, I put an altar below the painting and invited a *pujari* to come over and do *puja* to the painting. Often I would lie down and look at the painting in the candlelight. Sometimes I would ask her questions out loud. Once when I did that, I had a vision and the Divine Mother actually appeared to me in motion . . . and she showed me the future.

❧

That year the Divine Mother began really working with me. I was aware of it in many ways. Inside a cave in Machu Picchu, I received the instruction to go to Medjugorge, Yugoslavia, where the Virgin Mary was appearing to the children. I was told to go the day after Harmonic Convergence, and to go alone. This I did. Even though I am not Catholic and was unaware of any connection to the Virgin, I was aware of this much: That she must be an aspect of the Divine Mother and what was going on over there must be way beyond Catholicism. That experience was so profound that I wrote a whole book about it called *Inner Communion*.

Right after that I went to India to visit my teachers as usual. When I was at the home of Shastriji (Babaji's high priest), he did something very unusual with me which he had never done before and has never done since. He told me to sleep in "Babaji's bed" every night and report my dreams to him each morning. I always had the same dream. I dreamed that I was pregnant. Shastriji would always be ecstatic. I kept telling him that was not possible as I had been celibate by choice for quite some time. I had this dream four or five nights in a row. I could not figure it out. But then finally one yogi said to me, "Don't you get it . . . the Divine Mother impregnated you with her energy in the apparition room via the Virgin." I *had* felt her enter my uterus and I had almost fainted, as a matter of fact.

Because I had been so blessed in this incredible way, I felt it was very important that I share this energy with people. So I began telling others in my seminars about the experience. However, for the first months, I shook so much while trying to speak about it, I could hardly stand up. People could see that I was not shaking out of fear; but that some force of energy would take over my body. This created quite a reaction in the audience; and people would cry and/or go into spontaneous rebirthings. This reaction continued until after I wrote up the experience in *Inner Communion*, which, of course, helped me to integrate. However, when that book actually came out, I had such a shock seeing it that my body had a new and different reaction.

During that period I felt ready to go to the annual Divine Mother Festival in the Himalayas at Babaji's upper ashram. Babaji had said that one day at that event was equivalent to twelve years! That had seemed like impossible to me. Was he saying that you could make twelve years of spiritual progress in one day? How could that be? Was he saying that it would take twelve years of regular life on the outside to clear what you could clear there in one day? *Yes, he was.* I could hardly believe it, and yet Babaji would not make up something like that. Maybe I was afraid to believe it. What if it was true and what if I went there? Well, I finally did. And I finally knew it *was* true. I felt just like that . . . like you would go through twelve years of living in one day. It was the most intense experience of my life.

To have the privilege of being with those masters, those saints, those yogis, those *sadhus*, those beings who had come together to honor the Divine Mother was a highlight of my life. Imagine coming out of the Divine Mother temple and seeing the Himalayas right in front of you. Imagine being allowed to participate in the most ancient fire ceremonies that actually work on the elements. Imagine real miracles happening to people in front of your eyes. Imagine going to an ancient temple where the Divine Mother will heal you even of something like sterility. Shastriji said if you make it to that place and ask for a baby, the Divine Mother cannot refuse you, even if you have been sterile. Now again, I thought *that* was really too much. How could that be? But then it happened to one girl in my group who had that exact problem.

Every day the saints sit together and say prayers to the Divine Mother out loud. During this time, people in the temple would often have visions. After my first visit to the Divine Mother Festival, I began reading these prayers out loud myself before my altar. I remember the first time I did that. I was in Sweden. After I finished, the Divine Mother suddenly gave me a miracle. I "received" a fantastic new advanced wet rebirthing technique. I jumped into the bathtub and tried it and found it to be very very challenging. It took me several days to be able to really do it. I saw how incredible it would be for purification and rejuvenation. I was eager to try it on someone else. That year, when I took rebirthing to Russia, I was rebirthing my friend, Don McFarland, founder of Body Harmony, who had come along on the trip. I decided to tell him about it and he immediately wanted to try it. When he came up out of the water, he said, "*This* is a stroke of *genius*." "Well, I said, "It is from the Divine Mother."

❧

Later I designed a whole new training around this technique. I called it *The Liberation Training* and Don and I tried it out with a group of fifty people. We went to Iceland, the purest place we could find. The whole place is simply magic, with its glaciers, geysers, steam vents, volcanos, natural hot springs, and of course, the famous Blue Lagoon. Babaji had told us of the importance of meditation on the elements. I never really understood that until I worked in Iceland. The Divine Mother came through me like electricity itself. I actually felt electric currents running through my arms. The whole place felt like the Divine Mother ... and then, of course, I finally truly realized that the Divine Mother was the creative force itself. The life force itself. Then I understood why Shastriji had said to me once that the Divine Mother loved me so much. I had always loved life and so life loved me! It all made sense. Meditation on life ... it is the most potent meditation of all. And I saw how the Divine Mother had always been my teacher, my guru. And I saw how the Divine Mother was the guru of my guru. And I understood what the artist was talking about when she told me that Babaji had appeared to her when she was painting my painting. He appeared to her with his heart open and she said she saw the Divine Mother sitting in his heart.

Closing

A Vision in Sri Lanka

❦

A Course in Miracles says that Heaven is not a place, but rather a state of perfect oneness. I definitely had an experience of Heaven while writing this book. It happened in Sri Lanka, where I wrote the first draft. It happened the night before I started writing about Babaji.

I saw thousands of couples coming down toward me in the sky. Each person was obviously with his or her perfect mate. Each couple was in a state of perfection and so was their relationship, which I was able to somehow fully experience. Everyone looked exquisitely beautiful, joyous, and glowing. They seemed not only to be married couples, but also all "married" to everyone in the whole group. Then I heard the most glorious music I had ever heard in my life. It was from another dimension for sure; because it was nothing like anything I had ever heard before. It quite literally was "celestial." I had actually experienced Heaven.

For information about the India Quest trip:

John Paul and Sharda Collard
P.O. Box 515604
Dallas, TX 75251

———————

For more information on the Loving Relationship
Training, *please call us at our toll-free number*:

1-800-INTL-LRT
(1-800-468-5578)

Ashrams and Centers

United States

Bhole Baba Ashram
Box 461
Mountain View, Hawaii 86771
(808) 968-8737

The Haidakhandi Karma
    Yoga & Peace Center
Route 1, Box 60
Malmo, Nebraska 68040
(402) 642-9238

Consciousness Village
Campbell Hot Springs
Box 234
Sierraville, California 96126
(616) 994-8984

The Haidakhandi Universal
Ashram at Baia
Box 9
Crestone, Colorado 81131
(719) 256-4108

England

Hindu Center
Grafton Terrace 39
London NW5 G5
(19.44) 71/435.82.00

France

Centre De Babaji Pratima
Huguies
Salle de Cordagne, Apt. 1635
61.30.30.43

Foundation Spiritualle
D'Haidykhan
58 rue de la Liberte
38160 Soyssins (Grenoble)
78.21.35.94

Germany

Bhole Baba Ashram
Kalkstouk 11
5227 Rieferath D
(15.45) 2243/66.03

Baba Haidakhan Zentrum
Raifanberg 35
8551 Wailerebach D
(19.48) 8193/88.00

Holland

Babaji Center
Valentynkede 45
1095 JJ Amsterdam NL

India

Haidakhan Vishu'a Mahadham
via Kathgodam
District Nainital
26.3126
U.P. India
*Contact Gayatri at (401) 245-
5421 if you have further
questions.*

Italy

Centro Bhole Baba
Casella Postale 56
72014 Cisternino
Brindjial 1

Centro Spirituale Di Paos
  Hajdakhandi
Villa San Sacondo
Localita Monte Gaudio
ABTI 1

Bhole Baba Ghyan Ashram
Santa Maria di Pagialle
Pietrelunge (PG) 1

Centro Bhole Babba Ram
Via E. Gola 31
20100 Milano 1

Poland

Centrum Babadzigoo
U1. Zaporoska 54/12
Wroolaw P
(19.42) 71/51.22.97

Spain

Bhole Baba Ashram Vrindavana
46180 Liria E
(19.34) 96/275.30.17

Sweden

Haidakhan Baba Center
Nytorget 6   11640 Stockholm 2
(19.46) 8/540.51.79

Switzerland

Schweibenalp
3665 Brienz CH
(19.41) 35/61.20.01

DINOSAURS!

LORI STEIN

DINOSAURS!

Published by Liberty Street,
an imprint of Time Inc. Books,
a division of Meredith Corporation
225 Liberty Street
New York, NY 10281

LIBERTY
STREET

LIBERTY STREET is a trademark of Time Inc.

ISBN: 978-1-61893-186-3

First edition, 2016

2 QGV 18

10 9 8 7 6 5 4 3 2

Some of the content in this book was originally published in *Discovery Dinopedia: The Complete Guide to Everything Dinosaur.*

Produced by Scout Books & Media Inc

We welcome your comments and suggestions about Time Inc. Books. Please write to us at: Time Inc. Books, Attention: Book Editors, P.O. Box 62310, Tampa, FL 33662–2310
(800) 765-6400

timeincbooks.com

Time Inc. Books products may be purchased for business or promotional use. For information on bulk purchases, please contact Christi Crowley in the Special Sales Department at (845) 895-9858.

Dinosaur names are often long and hard to pronounce. The first time a dinosaur name is used, it appears in **bold**. You can find a guide to pronouncing all the dinosaur names in the book on page 110.

CONTENTS

DINO TIME! The Age of Dinosaurs lasted from 252 million to 66 million years ago. That's about 186 million years.

THE AGE OF DINOSAURS

For about 186 million years, a group of amazing creatures roamed our planet. This was the Age of Dinosaurs. There were thousands of different types of dinosaurs. They lived, ate, fought, and raised families. Some were huge—among the largest animals ever to live on Earth. Others were small. Fast or slow, fierce or gentle, they lived successfully for millions of years. They vanished about 66 million years ago. But dinosaurs left evidence that we can study to learn about them.

Dinosaurs lived in a world that is very different from Earth today. Our planet is about 4.6 billion years old. During the first few billion years, Earth's air had little oxygen. There was almost no life on the planet. Over time, the air became easier to breathe and small creatures appeared. The earliest known creatures lived in water. Some evolved to live on land. Then, dinosaurs appeared.

When dinosaurs became extinct (died out), their fossils remained. What is a fossil? Fossils can form when a creature dies in a place with the right amount of water and silt (bits of sand or clay in water). If this mixture buries the bones quickly, the skin and flesh rot away. The silt settles on the bones. This protects and preserves them. Bones can stay undisturbed this way for millions of years.

Scientists also learn a lot from coprolites (fossilized dinosaur poop), dinosaur eggs and nests, and tracks that were made by dinosaur feet. Sometimes,

WHAT IS EVOLUTION?

Evolution explains how living things change over time. Some dinosaurs were born with features that made them better able to survive. A dinosaur with a useful new feature passed that feature on to its babies. After thousands of years, dinosaurs without that feature died out.

in a place where a dinosaur rested or died, an outline of its body was left behind. These are ways we learn about dinosaurs and their world.

People have been discovering dinosaur bones for thousands of years. At first no one knew what they were. Some thought they might be the bones of dragons or giants. About 200 years ago, people began to recognize them as the bones of very large animals.

Scientists divide dinosaurs into two orders. The saurischian (lizard-hipped) and ornithischian (bird-hipped). These orders are divided again into groups. Dinosaurs in each group share common features.

One group in the

FOUND! These large fossilized dinosaur bones were uncovered on a dig.

saurischian order, called theropods, walked on two feet. They were the only dinosaurs that were carnivores—they ate meat. Theropods range from huge predators, such as ***Tyrannosaurus rex,*** which hunted other animals, to small, birdlike creatures such as ***Troodon***.

Troodon

Brachiosaurus

The sauropod group were also saurischians. They walked on four legs and were herbivores. They ate plants. Sauropods include **Brachiosaurus** and **Apatosaurus**. These dinosaurs grew very large and moved slowly. They had small heads and brains.

The ornithischian order of dinosaurs includes thyreophorans, ornithopods, and marginocephalians. Thyreophorans were large and heavy. They had bony plates on their bodies. **Stegosaurus** and

Ankylosaurus

Ankylosaurus are two types. They walked on four legs and ate plants.

Hadrosaurus

The dinosaurs in the ornithopod group also ate plants. They switched from walking on four legs when they were looking for food to running on two legs to escape a predator. *Iguanodon* and *Hadrosaurus* are in this group.

The maginocephalian group includes dinosaurs with pointed horns, such as *Triceratops*. Dinosaurs such as *Stegoceras* belong in this group, too. They all walked on four legs and ate plants.

Triceratops

WE'VE GOT YOUR SIZE

People think of dinosaurs as huge animals. Some of them were the largest to ever walk on land. But dinosaurs came in every size. The largest was as tall as a four-story building. The smallest was the size of a chicken. Here's how six popular dinos stack up.

A

B

Humans average 5.5 feet in height

Length from tip of snout to tip of tail

A Over 40 feet: *Brachiosaurus*

B 30–40 feet: *Yangchuanosaurus*

C 20–30 feet: *Stegosaurus*

WHAT MAKES A DINOSAUR A DINOSAUR?

HARD AND SOFT PALATE The palate is the roof of the mouth. The shape of dinosaurs' palates allowed the animals to eat and breathe at the same time.

HOLES IN THE HEAD Dinosaur skulls had three pairs of openings, not counting the eyes and nostrils.

HOLE IN THE HIP Every dinosaur had a hole through each hip socket.

STOOD UPRIGHT Whether they walked on two or four legs, dinosaurs stood upright. Their legs were directly beneath their bodies.

D 10–20 feet: *Zuniceratops*

E 5–10 feet: *Deinonychus*

F Under 5 feet: *Archaeopteryx*

Experts divide time on our planet into long spans called eras. There are four eras: Precambrian, Paleozoic, Mesozoic, and Cenozoic. Dinosaurs lived during the Mesozoic Era. Within this era, there are three periods of time. These periods mark when different dinosaurs lived and died out.

During the Triassic Period (252 million to 201 million years ago), the first dinosaurs appeared in what is now South America. They were mostly small carnivores. Triassic dinosaurs include *Coelophysis*, *Eoraptor*, and *Herrerasaurus*.

The Jurassic Period (201 million to 144 million years ago), was a time when huge dinosaurs ruled the world. There were small furry animals. Flowering plants became food for herbivores. Some Jurassic dinosaurs are **Dilophosaurus**, **Massospondylus**, **Dryosaurus**, **Allosaurus**, *Apatosaurus*, **Diplodocus**, and *Stegosaurus*.

Dinosaurs continued to dominate in the Cretaceous Period (144 million to 66 million years ago). Cretaceous dinosaurs include *Deinonychus*, **Psittacosaurus**, **Parasaurolophus**, *Triceratops*, and *Tyrannosaurus rex*.

Then, 66 million years ago, dinosaurs became extinct. No one knows exactly why. It was probably because a huge asteroid hit Earth.

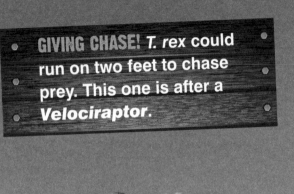

GIVING CHASE! *T. rex* could run on two feet to chase prey. This one is after a **Velociraptor.**

WHEN "BEAST FEET" WALKED THE EARTH

Theropods lived throughout the entire Age of Dinosaurs. The earliest known dinosaurs were theropods, and theropods were still around when the dinosaurs vanished 66 million years ago. The name *theropod* comes from two Greek words that mean "beast feet." When the largest theropods stomped around, the ground trembled. Smaller animals would have run away.

Many theropods had birdlike bodies

with hollow bones. This made them light and fast. Others, including *Tyrannosaurus rex*, were heavy and slow. All of them had big, sharp teeth for eating meat. They had large eyes and large brains that helped them hunt and avoid attacks.

Paleontologists have found 267 kinds of theropods. Their fossils have been found everywhere in the world.

Theropods came in many different sizes, from less than 3 feet to more than 45 feet long. Some had long, curving necks, and tails and jaws shaped like a crocodile's. Others had shorter necks, tails, and snouts. They all walked on two feet, ate meat, and had hollow bones. Early theropods were smaller and less fierce than the ones that came later. But they still had very sharp teeth and claws, strong legs, and hollow bones that made them light enough to run quickly. These animals include *Herrerasaurus* and **Tawa**, which lived during the Late Triassic Period.

Over millions of years, dinosaurs became bigger and deadlier. Small changes in their bodies, such as sharper claws and stronger tails,

WHICH DINOSAURS WERE THE SMARTEST?

Paleontologists think *Troodon* was as smart as modern raptors, such as eagles and hawks. *Deinonychus* was also intelligent, and probably hunted in groups.

made them better predators. Some of the most famous meat eaters, such as *Allosaurus*, **Spinosaurus**, and **Carcharodontosaurus**, were the top predators of their time. They ate other animals, but no other animals ate them! They were also among the biggest theropods that ever lived.

Allosaurus had a special jaw joint so it could open its mouth super wide and hold huge chunks of flesh. It also had bony ridges over each eye that may have worked like sunshades.

Spinosaurus had powerful jaws like a crocodile's,

Allosaurus

with sharp teeth
and a 6-foot-high,
fan-shaped sail on its
back. Scientists think it
may have used
the sail to control

Spinosaurus

its temperature by absorbing or
releasing body heat. Or it may have
used it to signal other dinosaurs.

Carcharodontosaurus had a massive
body and tail. Its head was 5 feet long
and its sharp teeth were 8 inches long.
It was bigger than *Tyrannosaurus rex*.

From the Late Jurassic Period
to the Late Cretaceous Period, many
new dinosaurs appeared. Although the
dinosaurs in this group looked different
from one another, they all had stiff tails

and feathers of some sort. Some of them (such as ***Ornithomimus***) became more like birds. Others (such as *Tyrannosaurus rex*) became bigger and deadlier. They were called tyrant dinosaurs. A tyrant is a creature that uses power to control weaker creatures.

Many kinds of tyrant dinosaurs lived in North America and Asia at the end of the Cretaceous Period. Most of the tyrant dinosaurs were the biggest and strongest animals in their environment. They fought and ate other animals.

They had massive skulls, sharp teeth,
small arms, and big tails,
which helped them balance.
One of the last groups of
theropods were near-raptors, which
looked a lot like birds. They are closely

TYRANT TEETH

Tyrant dinosaurs had lots of big, sharp teeth.
As many as 70 teeth lined their jaws and gave
them a frightening appearance. Their teeth
had tiny cracks, but these cracks didn't make
them weaker. The cracks helped distribute
pressure along the jaws. This meant the
tyrants could bite with tremendous force
without breaking their teeth.

related to predator birds, such as eagles and hawks. The near-raptor dinosaurs were covered with feathers. Their arm bones were similar to wing bones.

Velociraptor

Many near-raptors ate plants. They probably chopped them off with their claws and beaked jaws.

Most near-raptors were less than 10 feet tall. *Therizinosaurus* was an exception. At almost 40 feet long, it was one of the biggest theropods. Many near-raptors, such as *Oviraptor*, were found in Asia, and some have been found in North and South America. *Deinonychus* and *Velociraptor* were also birdlike dinosaurs. They were vicious and may have hunted in packs.

Fossils can reveal fascinating stories about how dinosaurs lived and died.

Ghost Ranch is an area in New Mexico where many dinosaur fossils have been found. Hundreds of *Coelophysis* skeletons were discovered in huge, tangled piles. In the Triassic Period, this area was located near the Equator. Scientists think heavy rains could have caused flash floods that drowned a whole pack of these dinosaurs.

Coelophysis

Big Al

When a team of paleontologists found a nearly complete *Allosaurus* skeleton in Wyoming in 1991, at first they thought it was an adult dinosaur. But when they looked closer, they realized it was probably an adolescent. The bones told the story of the difficult life this young dinosaur had. It had lost limbs, broken ribs and other bones, and suffered infections. The scientists named the skeleton "Big Al" and wrote its life story. Later, a television show called *The Ballad of Big Al* showed its life from birth to death.

CRUNCH THIS! *T. rex*'s bite was the strongest of any animal that ever lived.

CHAPTER
3

T. REX: THE KING OF DINOSAURS

Tyrannosaurus rex means "tyrant lizard king," and this dinosaur lived up to its name. It was a powerful and vicious ruler of the planet. *T. rex* was a theropod dinosaur, which means it walked on two feet and ate meat. It was a top predator. Its sharp teeth and powerful 4-foot-long jaw could crunch through bone and rip apart flesh. *T. rex* wasn't the largest dinosaur, but it was the biggest carnivore of its day. It grew up to 40 feet long and weighed up to 15,000 pounds. That's as long as a school bus and as heavy as nine polar bears.

T. rex was one of the last dinosaurs to appear, about 2 million years before all dinosaurs became extinct. Like other theropods, *T. rex* had an enormous skull, strong teeth and claws, small arms, and a big tail. *T. rex*'s awesome body and physical abilities made it the most deadly dinosaur of its day.

It had powerful back legs and could run in an upright position. The sharp claws on its small hands and big feet could catch, hold, and rip apart prey (animals to eat). Its short arms would not have helped it attack other dinosaurs. But some experts think those arms were very strong. They were used to grip live prey, while the jaws worked on tearing flesh.

Good vision allowed *T. rex* to spot prey or other animals looking to fight over something (maybe a mate or food). It had deep eye sockets and eyes pointing straight ahead. These gave *T. rex* better

DID ANYONE BATTLE T. REX?

T. rex didn't have an easy life. It lived in a dino-eat-dino world. Fossils show that *T. rex* was gored by horned dinosaurs that were defending themselves. It also lost limbs in fights and was sometimes attacked by other *T. rexes*.

PINOCCHIO REX

NOSE FOR NEWS

In the spring of 2014, paleontologists in China found a smaller cousin of *T. rex* that had a long snout. They officially named it **Qianzhousaurus**, but commonly call it "Pinocchio rex" after its impressive nose. It's a theropod *Tyrannosaurus* like *T. rex*. It was about 29 feet long—including its super long snout.

depth perception than dinosaurs with eyes pointing to the sides, so it could see how far away something was. *T. rex* had much bigger eyes than a human, so its vision was probably better than ours.

By examining the size of its nose, scientists can tell that *T. rex* had the best sense of smell of any dinosaur.

It could find something to eat by smelling it from far away.

T. rex's teeth were 8 to 9 inches long. There were more than 50 of them in its massive jaws. Each tooth was cone-shaped, curved, and strong enough to crunch through bones. The teeth were not super sharp. Instead, they were

ALWAYS A HUNTER?

In 2013, scientists found a *T. rex* tooth in a fossil of a duckbilled dinosaur's tailbone. This proves that *T. rex* hunted and killed its food. But some paleontologists think *T. rex* was also a scavenger. It might have looked for dead animals to eat instead of always killing live ones. Finding and killing a big dinosaur, such as *Triceratops*, could have fed a *T. rex* for several weeks. But eating a dead animal it found would have taken less energy and been less dangerous.

T. rex used its strong bite to kill and eat prey.

solid and could chomp down on animals of any size.

T. rex's bite was three times as strong as a great white shark's or a crocodile's, and 60 times as strong as a human's. It had the strongest bite of any animal that ever lived. The bite was strong because its teeth were big and solid. Plus, its skull and jaws were enormous, and it could open its mouth very wide.

T. rex fossils are usually found alone. This means they probably were loners and didn't hunt in packs.

How smart was *T. rex*? Scientists measure a dinosaur's intelligence by comparing the size of its brain to the size of its body. By that measurement, *T. rex* is one of the smartest dinosaurs.

The largest, best-preserved, and most complete *Tyrannosaurus rex* skeleton ever discovered is nicknamed "Sue." Sue's skeleton was found in the Badlands of South Dakota. It has been put together, and now is on display in the Field Museum in Chicago.

This remarkable find even includes the tiny bones of the inner ear, which have rarely been found with T. rex skeletons. By studying the bones in Sue's skull that were around its brain, scientists made a fascinating discovery: A large part of Sue's brain was used to recognize smells.

Since the exhibit opened in May 2000, more than 16 million people have visited Sue. So far, no one knows whether Sue was male or female. The skeleton was named for the paleontologist who discovered it, Sue Hendrickson.

Sue's discovery was a happy accident. Several researchers were ready to drive home from a field trip when their car got a flat tire. Most of the group went to a nearby town to have the tire repaired. But Sue Hendrickson decided to stay behind and look around a site that the group hadn't explored. She looked up from the base of a cliff and saw a few bones stuck in the rocks about 8 feet above her head. The bones were big enough to go have a look.

Sue is more than 42 feet long.
The bones weigh 3,922 pounds.

GROWTH CURVE! An ***Argentinosaurus*** egg was the size of a coconut. It grew 25,000 times its hatchling size to become an adult.

BABIES, FAMILIES, AND HERDS

How did dinosaurs begin their lives? Even the biggest, deadliest dinosaur started out as a baby hatched from an egg. Many types of dinosaurs went through a time where they needed their parents to take care of them, like human babies do. Others were able to care for themselves right after they were born. From fossils, scientists have learned a great deal about how dinosaur babies were born and how they grew up.

Dinosaurs had a special way of finding mates and having babies. For example, an *Eoraptor* male built a nest and showed it to a female. A good nest was important for having a family. Some experts think this was one of the ways to attract a mate. Later, the female laid eggs in the nest. Dinosaurs laid many eggs at a time.

Some dinosaurs, such as **Gigantoraptor**, sat on their nests. This is called brooding. It's a way to keep eggs warm at night and cool during the day. This steady, even source of heat helped the eggs develop properly. Modern birds, which are closely related to dinosaurs, also brood. Bigger dinosaurs, too heavy to sit on their eggs, may have covered them with plants to keep them warm.

Finally, the eggs cracked open. What happened to the baby dinosaurs after they hatched from their shells? Many dinosaur parents took care of their babies. Young dinosaurs often stayed in their nests for a few months or even longer. And even after they left the nest, some dinosaurs hung around with their siblings.

Many young dinosaurs learned how to find food by hunting or foraging (finding plant food) with their parents. The parents showed their babies how to look for food, and protected them when predators came near.

Some fossils of young dinosaurs were found near both male and female adults. This might mean dinosaur fathers stayed around to care for their young. In Cody, Wyoming, 20 adult and young *Drinker* dinosaurs were found together in a hole, with the adults on top of the children. Scientists think the parents pushed their children into the hole to escape a predator.

Dinosaurs grew slowly for the first few years of their lives—and then grew very large, very fast. By the time it reached the age of ten, a *Tyrannosaurus rex* weighed about 1,000 pounds. In the next few years, it grew 1,000 pounds each year. When it reached its adult weight of 12,000 pounds, it stopped growing. Different kinds of

FACT FILE: NESTING NOTES

For many years, scientists thought dinosaurs hatched from eggs, but were not sure. How did they find out for sure? In 1978, paleontologist Jack Horner discovered some fossilized dinosaur nests, eggshells, and embryos in Montana. From this important find, we learned how dinosaurs made their nests, cared for their eggs, and fed their babies after they were hatched.

Model of a Maiasaura nest

dinosaurs grew up in different ways. Some, such as *Argentinosaurus*, were able to take care of themselves as soon as they were born. They learned to move around, find food, and avoid being attacked.

Some dinosaurs lived in groups called herds. They hunted, ate, and traveled together. Many animals live in herds today, including elephants, antelopes, and buffalo.

Paleontologists believe dinosaurs that lived in herds behaved the way modern herd animals do. It's possible there were leaders, followers, and battles for position. Dinosaur nests have been found grouped together. Giving birth was sometimes part of herd life. Protecting young, sick, and old members from attack was another herd activity.

Argentinosaurus herd

EASY GLIDER *Archaeopteryx* was covered with feathers. They were not spaced the right way for strong, fast flight. This means it probably did more gliding than flying.

LOOK! UP IN THE SKY!

Where did modern birds come from? At one time, scientists believed that they came from large flying reptiles called pterosaurs. Then they thought a winged theropod dinosaur might be the first bird. But many other theropod dinosaurs had birdlike features and did not fly. Experts now agree that modern birds evolved from these theropod dinosaurs. There's much more still to discover about how dinosaurs evolved into flying animals.

In 1861, a small animal that looked like a raven was discovered in a fossil bed in Germany. This new creature was called *Archaeopteryx*. Was it a bird or a dinosaur? Paleontologists have debated this question for a long time. Some experts said *Archaeopteryx* was the first bird. It had wings and feathers, and probably could fly. Most experts agree that *Archaeopteryx* was a link between dinosaurs and birds. It was part dinosaur and part bird.

The ancestors of birds included *Deinonychus*, *Oviraptor*, and *Velociraptor*. These smart carnivores walked on two legs, like birds. Their arms were short, but the bones in them were similar to wings. They had feathers but did not fly. At some point, their bird descendants lifted off the ground. How that happened is still a mystery.

SIMILAR TRAITS

Dinosaurs had feathers! They first appeared on theropods about 150 million years ago. Pretty feathers might have helped attract a mate.

Some dinosaurs, such as *Velociraptor*, had sharp claws. These helped catch and hold prey while eating.

Theropods walked on two legs. So do birds. In fact, since birds evolved from theropod dinosaurs, you can call them living dinosaurs.

WHAT WERE THEY?

Pterosaurs were large flying reptiles that lived during the Age of Dinosaurs. But they weren't dinosaurs. Until about 50 years ago, some scientists believed birds evolved from pterosaurs or a close relative. But now all agree that they evolved from theropod dinosaurs.

Quetzalcoatlus

Anhanguera was a pterosaur from the Early Cretaceous Period. It had a wingspan of 15 feet. Its legs were weak. It probably spent very little time on the ground. *Quetzalcoatlus* was a pterosaur from the Late Cretaceous Period. It had the largest wingspan—around 36 feet—of any known animal. It probably pushed off with both front and back legs. Its wings worked like sails on a boat.

But pterosaurs did not have feathers. Their skeletons do not resemble the skeletons of modern birds. When scientists compared bird skeletons to dinosaur fossils, they discovered something surprising: Birds evolved from fast theropod dinosaurs called near-raptors and paravians.

BIG AND TALL *Brachiosaurus* means "arm lizard." Its arms were longer than its legs.

GENTLE GIANTS

Sauropods were huge plant-eating dinosaurs. The name sauropod comes from a Greek word meaning "lizard feet." Most had similar features: an enormous body, four thick legs, and lizardlike feet with claws. Their big size helped them scare away predators. Big stomachs gave them extra storage space for food. There are 198 known sauropods—about ten times as many as theropods. Sauropod fossils have been found on all seven continents.

The first sauropods appeared in the Late Triassic Period, more than 200 million years ago. Some of the earliest ones ate meat and walked on two legs. Early sauropods were large compared to other animals of the time. But they were smaller than the giants that followed.

Eoraptor is one of the earliest dinosaurs identified as a sauropod. It was small, weighed about 20 pounds, and ate meat. *Massospondylus* could walk on both two and four feet. It was 13 to 20 feet long and weighed about 300 pounds. It was an omnivore. It ate both meat and plants.

Vulcanodon, an herbivore, lived in the Early Jurassic Period, about 200 million to 180 million years ago. It walked on

four feet and weighed about 8,000 pounds. That's as much as two cars.

Over millions of years, the earliest sauropods evolved into gigantic dinosaurs—the largest animals that ever walked on land. As they grew

Eoraptors

BIG BABIES

HIGH TECH DATA

Scientists are using modern equipment like CT scanners and computer models to understand how sauropods grew so big. They found that the babies grew super fast. Hatchlings went from 7 pounds to 80 pounds in about eight weeks.

bigger, they needed to walk on all four legs to support their weight. Their diet shifted to only plants.

By the Middle Jurassic Period, starting around 180 million years ago, they had super long necks and tails, and small heads. There were big nostrils on the tops of their heads.

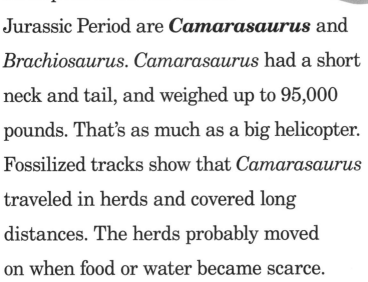

Two of the most famous sauropods from the Middle Jurassic Period are ***Camarasaurus*** and *Brachiosaurus. Camarasaurus* had a short neck and tail, and weighed up to 95,000 pounds. That's as much as a big helicopter. Fossilized tracks show that *Camarasaurus* traveled in herds and covered long distances. The herds probably moved on when food or water became scarce.

Brachiosaurus's arms were longer than its legs by more than a foot. (*Brachia* means "arms.") This huge dinosaur walked on all four limbs, so its shoulders and neck were higher than its back. It would have been able to reach the tops of the trees without stretching its long neck.

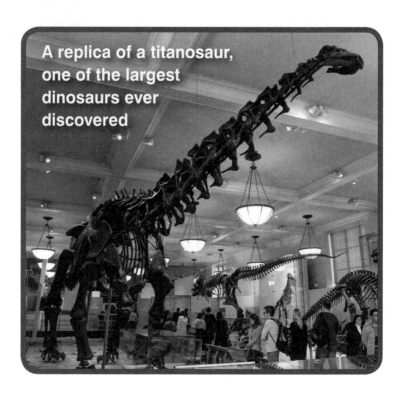

A replica of a titanosaur, one of the largest dinosaurs ever discovered

Titanosaurs were a group of very large dinosaurs that appeared in the Cretaceous Period. (*Titan* means "giant.") They lived until dinosaurs disappeared 66 million years ago. There may have been more than 100 different types

of dinosaurs in this group.
They include some of the largest
dinosaurs ever discovered.

One of the titanosaurs, *Argentinosaurus*,
was about 115 feet long and weighed
more than 146,000 pounds. An
Argentinosaurus egg was the size of
a coconut. A baby grew 25,000 times
its hatchling size to become an adult.

Whiptail dinosaurs had a very long
neck, a whiplike tail, and a huge body
with a big belly on short legs. Some
of the biggest and most well-known
dinosaurs were in the whiptail group,
including *Apatosaurus* and *Diplodocus*.
They grew to more than 100 feet long
and had some of longest necks and tails
of all animals.

FACT FILE: APATOSAURUS

***Apatosaurus* was one of the largest** animals to ever live on land. It is also one of the most popular dinosaurs of all time. It was very strong and heavily built. Its vertebrae (the bones in its spine) were arranged so it could hold its tail above the ground to maintain balance.

Its name means "deceptive lizard." That means it seems to be something it is not. When it was first discovered, experts found that some of its bones were similar to those of reptiles. But they determined that *Apatosaurus* was really a dinosaur.

For about 100 years, *Apatosaurus* was called ***Brontosaurus***. Why was the name changed? Fossil hunter O.C. Marsh discovered two dinosaur skeletons a long time ago. He named the first one *Apatosaurus* and the second one *Brontosaurus*. Neither skeleton had its head attached. (Sauropod skulls are lightly attached to their bodies and often rolled away.)

For a while scientists thought they had two different dinosaurs. Later, paleontologists studying the bones realized that they were the same animal. The first name, *Apatosaurus*, is the one that stuck.

Apatosaurus skull

• DINO DETAIL •

BODY OF THE BEAST

Experts have a good idea about how dinosaur bones fit together because some full skeletons have been found. This *T. rex* model is one example.

TAIL was long and heavy.

LIZARD-HIPPED

LEGS AND FEET were built for running.

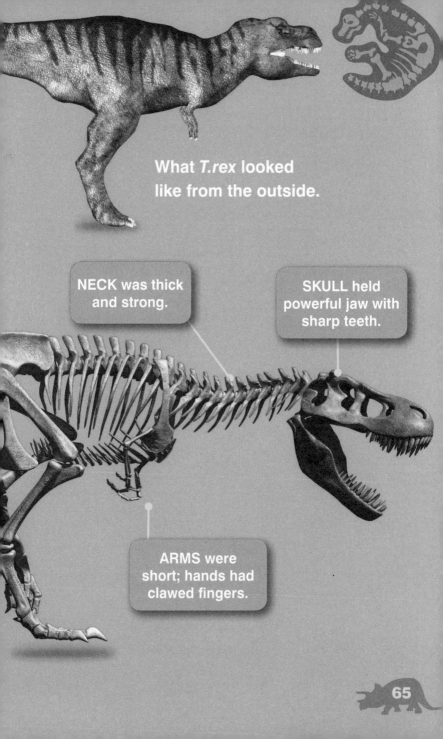

What *T. rex* looked
like from the outside.

NECK was thick
and strong.

SKULL held
powerful jaw with
sharp teeth.

ARMS were
short; hands had
clawed fingers.

HEADS UP! Herbivores, like this *Brachiosaurus*, were browsers. This means they chomped on leaves and other vegetation.

WHAT'S FOR DINNER?

Dinosaurs chose different kinds of food. They ate and digested it in different ways, too. About one-eighth of all dinosaurs were carnivores that ate small mammals, reptiles, and other dinosaurs. Most of the rest were herbivores, which ate plants. There were also a few insectivores, which ate bugs, and piscivores, which ate fish. Some dinosaurs were not choosy about their food and ate everything—small reptiles and mammals, insects, fish, and plants. These are called omnivores. (*Omni* means "all.")

Dinosaurs had different ways of eating. Each had the right teeth for its diet. Carnivores had long, sharp teeth, like a lion's. They used them to catch and rip up other animals. Carnivore teeth could tear off chunks of meat or the dinosaur could eat small animals whole.

Rounded, dull herbivore teeth stripped leaves off bark. Many plant-eating dinosaurs, such as ***Styracosaurus*** and *Triceratops*, had extra sets of teeth in their cheeks. These were used to grind the plants they ate into a mush that could be digested. But most dinosaur teeth and jaws were not designed for chewing. Instead, the food was swallowed in large chunks and broken down in the stomach.

Spinosaurus ate fish.

HERBIVORE TEETH VS CARNIVORE TEETH

Flat, dull teeth allowed herbivores to grind up the leaves and plants they ate.

Sharp, pointy teeth helped meat-eaters kill and rip apart other animals.

Plants have few calories, which are the units of energy in food. To get enough energy to keep their big bodies nourished, plant eaters had to spend most of their time eating.

Large herbivores needed a huge stomach to hold and break down all the plants they ate. Experts think most of these dinosaurs had a special chamber in their stomach. In this chamber, stomach acids would break down the plants. Then the nutrients could be absorbed.

When we think of meat-eating dinosaurs, we might imagine them constantly ripping other dinosaurs apart and eating them. It is true that carnivores attacked big herbivores and other carnivores. Some even ate others of their own species. But dinosaurs also ate small mammals, birds, and reptiles. We know this because fossilized remains of small animals have been found in the rib cages of meat-eating dinosaurs.

DINO DETAIL

THE SCOOP ON POOP

Coprolite is a fancy word for poop
fossil. Paleontologists have found many
well-preserved piles of coprolites. By
analyzing these poop fossils, they can
tell if they came from herbivores or
carnivores. They can learn a lot about
the plant life of a certain time period by

matching dinosaur skeletons to the types of plants in their poop.

Some plant eaters found a way to help their digestive system break down woody or tough plants. They swallowed small rocks called gastroliths. These rocks mashed up the food in their stomachs every time they moved. A few dinosaur skeletons have been found with these rocks in the place where the stomach would have been.

Fossilized dino poop

SLOW MOVER *Kentrosaurus* had a small head, a toothless beak for tearing leaves, and body armor for protection.

READY FOR BATTLE

Thyreophorans, also called armored dinosaurs, were among the first dinosaurs of the Early Jurassic Period. They were heavy, slow-moving herbivores. Some were just a few feet long. Others were almost 40 feet long. Thyreophorans had awesome protective body armor. Dinosaurs in one group, called stegosaurs, had bony plates running along their backs. Ankylosaurs were covered in bony plates that were raised, like large bumps, along their bodies. They all had small heads and tiny brains. They were not the smartest dinosaurs, but they were tough.

Thyreophoran fossils have been found on all seven continents, but they are most common in the western United States. There are 80 known thyreophorans. The name thyreophoran comes from Greek and means "shield bearer."

Many stegosaurs had two rows of spikes sticking out of their plates. Predators were less likely to attack stegosaurs since even sharp teeth couldn't bite the plates. All the stegosaurs walked on four feet. They had hard beaks that they used to snip leaves

Stegosaurus

and twigs off low-growing plants.

Stegosaurus is the best known of the stegosaur group. The protection of bony plates was important for a dinosaur that moved slowly and wasn't tough or intelligent. At up to 40 feet long, *Stegosaurus* was about ten times the size of a dog. But its brain was only one-quarter the size of a dog's brain.

Gigantspinosaurus

Gigantspinosaurus had
two gigantic spines, or spikes,
that stuck out of its shoulders.
Kentrosaurus had bony plates on its
neck and back, and two rows of spikes
along its tail. Experts think the plates
helped members of a herd identify each
other. Their spiked tails, however, were
excellent defensive weapons.

Ankylosaurs, also called armored lizards, were built like tanks and had fused (connected) bony plates all over their bodies. The earliest species, such as **Polacanthus** and **Nodosaurus**, were covered in light plates and thin spikes. *Nodosaurus* had a soft belly. It may have dropped down and hugged the ground to protect itself when attacked.

Minmi, another early kind of ankylosaur, was a nibbler. It bit off tiny parts of plants rather than swallowing them whole. Small bits of plants were found in the stomach of a well-preserved *Minmi* fossil.

Ankylosaurus, which evolved later in the Early Cretaceous Period, had a very heavy

Ankylosaurus

body on short, thick legs. *Ankylosaurus* weighed more than 8,000 pounds when fully grown. Even the biggest carnivores could not have tipped it over to get to its soft belly. And their big, sharp teeth wouldn't have been able to pierce the heavy armor.

FACT FILE: TAIL TALES

Thyreophorans' tails could be aimed at predators and used for attack.

Many stegosaurs had tails with four spikes arranged in a pattern. Tests with models of these spikes show that a tail like this would have been an effective weapon. *Stegosaurus* had the muscles to swing its tail hard at an attacker.

Stegosaurus

The club at the end of a young *Ankylosaurus*'s tail was as big and heavy as a bowling ball. As the dinosaur got older, the club would have grown even bigger. A hard thwack from that tail could have broken the bones of a predator.

Ankylosaurus

HEADWAY *Parasaurolophus* was named for the long, backward-facing crest on its head (*para* means "beside" and *lophos* means "crest" in Greek).

SPEED RACERS

Ornithopods were not the biggest or the smartest or the most vicious dinosaurs. But they had several very useful features. Most could walk on either four feet or two feet, depending on whether they were eating or running. They were good at chewing and could get a lot of nutrition from their food. Some had duckbills for snipping plants and thumb spikes to gather food. Because of these advantages, ornithopods grew in size and in number.

The name ornithopod comes from two Greek words meaning "bird feet." Most of these dinosaurs had feet with three toes, like birds. There are 130 known ornithopods, and their fossils have been found everywhere in the world.

Ornithopods play a huge role in the history of fossil hunting. The first plant-eating dinosaur to be officially named was an ornithopod called *Iguanodon*. The first nests of dinosaur eggs found belonged to the ornithopod **Maiasaura**. The first nearly complete dinosaur skeleton ever found was another ornithopod, *Hadrosaurus*. It was found on a farm in Haddonfield, New Jersey, in 1858. The first fossilized dinosaur

skin discovered was attached
to the skeleton of an ornithopod
called **_Edmontosaurus_**.

Ornithopods had interlocking rows
of teeth. All those teeth allowed them to
chew their food thoroughly. This meant
they could break down tough plants
for easier digestion and to get the most
nutrients. As teeth wore down, new ones
moved into their place.

Many ornithopods had thumb spikes.
These were up to 6 inches long and very
thick. The thumb spikes would have been
good weapons against predators. Some
scientists think they were most useful for
breaking up fruit and gathering food, like
a built-in knife.

Ornithopods could also walk on four

feet while eating, and then stand on two legs and run fast. Some, such as *Dryosaurus*, had strong legs that would have given it speed to escape predators.

Big, bulky *Iguanodon* had all the ornithopod advantages. It could switch from running on two legs to walking on four legs. It had many teeth to chew its food thoroughly. And it had big thumb spikes to do many jobs. The front of its beak was toothless, but it had 29 big teeth in each cheek. Its beak was sharp enough to snip off plants, and its cheeks were

Iguanodon

big enough to hold food while the
teeth ground it up. *Iguanodon*
also had a flexible pinkie finger to help
it grab and gather food. These eating aids
helped it grow to about 30 feet
long and 9 feet tall. In fact, it
was one of the biggest ornithopods.
Using its size and its thumb spikes, it
could survive fights with carnivores.

A group of ornithopods called
hadrosaurs lived in the forests of

Maiasaura

Europe, Asia, and North America in the Late Cretaceous Period. Their common name is duckbill, because the heads of some members resembled those of modern ducks. They had long, flat bills or short beaks that were just right for snipping twigs and leaves from trees.

Hadrosaurs were big, sturdy dinosaurs with all the helpful body parts of ornithopods. They also had horns, spikes, and crests. This headgear may have been only for show. But experts think it may have been used to attract mates or help the dinosaurs make louder sounds.

FACT FILE: SKIN AND BONES

In 1999, a 16-year-old amateur paleontologist named Tyler Lyson was searching for fossils on his uncle's farm in North Dakota. Lyson made an amazing discovery: a mummified Edmontosaurus skeleton. (Mummification is a process that dries and preserves skin.) The skeleton was almost whole, with the skin attached.

Lyson and a group of experts carefully dug up the skeleton. They named it "Dakota" and spent years studying it. The mummified skin showed bumps rather than scales. It may have had a striped pattern.

Lyson's discovery, on display at the North Dakota Heritage Center

MAKING A POINT *Styracosaurus* had four to six horns on its neck frill, one on each cheek, and one on its beak. It had short legs, and experts think it may have run up to 20 miles per hour.

CALL THEM "BIG HEADS"

They weren't known for their speed, size, or intelligence. But the dinosaur group called marginocephalians, or fringe heads, were definitely not ordinary. There were two kinds of dinosaurs in the group.

Horn-face dinosaurs, or ceratopsians, include *Triceratops* and its relatives. They had pointy horns all over their heads. Some also had sharp spikes sticking out and large frills that grew

Triceratops, a horn-faced dinosaur, had horns, frills, and ridges.

out of their skulls. Another group, called dome-heads, had thick caps of bone on their heads. All of the marginocephalian dinosaurs walked on four legs and they all ate plants.

Marginocephalian fossils have been found in Europe, Asia, and North America. There are 85 known marginocephalians.

These dinosaurs had other important features besides their horns. They had strong bodies and many teeth that were good for eating plants. Their tough beaks may have been covered in a hard protective coating called keratin, which is also found in human skin, hair, and nails.

When they were young, horn-face dinosaurs basically looked alike. Their horns changed shape and size as they grew older. Some horns vanished and others grew in. Adults had horns, frills, and spikes that were different from each other's.

Psittacosaurus was named for its head, which was like a parrot's (*psittakos* means "parrot" in Greek). It had teeth and a beak that could chop off plants.

Triceratops was one of the late arrivals on the dinosaur scene. It didn't appear until 69 million years ago—about 3 million years before all dinosaurs became extinct. It lived around the same time as *Tyrannosaurus rex*. Skeletons of both dinosaurs have been found with scars from battles between them. *Triceratops* was a big, heavy animal with a huge skull. How huge? Its head was about one-third the length of its whole body! Topping off its skull was an enormous frill, which pointed backward and extended up to 7 feet.

Paleontologists think the tight, bony domes of dome-head dinosaurs were used to butt one another in the sides when competing for mates.

Dome-head dinosaurs grew to only about 15 feet at their longest. They appeared in the Late Cretaceous Period. Mostly, they roamed western North America, as far east as New Mexico. Some have also been found in Asia.

Pachycephalosaurus had a bony skull that was more than 10 inches thick. Experts think it was used to head-butt rivals and predators. *Stegoceras* had large, forward-facing eye sockets. That may mean it had binocular vision, which helped it focus and know how far away something was.

Pachycephalosaurus

FACT FILE: FIGHTING

In 1971, two skeletons were found in the Gobi Desert, their limbs locked in battle. They were a *Velociraptor* and a **Protoceratops**. Scientists think the two were fighting when a sandstorm killed them both. Although the fossils show the battle, we have to guess which dinosaur would have won.

Velociraptor was a theropod. It weighed about 40 pounds and was about 6 feet long. It had big, sharp claws and small, pointy teeth, and it moved quickly. Although it was not the most intelligent dinosaur, it was still pretty smart.

Protoceratops was a ceratopsian herbivore. It was about 6 feet long and weighed about 400 pounds. It had a small frill on its head and a hard beak. It was slow and had a very small brain.

It looks as though the *Protoceratops* has a grip on the *Velociraptor* in the illustration below. Which one do you think would have won the battle?

Protoceratops fighting a
Velociraptor.

WHAT HAPPENED? A huge natural change wiped out the dinosaurs. Scientists are studying exactly what occurred.

AN END AND A BEGINNING

Until 66 million years ago, dinosaurs wandered all over the planet. Big carnivores such as *T. rex* dominated. New species, including *Triceratops*, popped up. Then the fossil record shows they all became extinct. There is great debate about what kind of disaster killed the dinosaurs.

Most scientists think a huge asteroid from space hit Earth, creating tsunamis— giant tidal waves—and dust clouds.

Scientists have found a mineral called iridium in soil that dates back to the time of the dinosaur extinction. Iridium is rare on Earth, but there is plenty in asteroids. A truly massive asteroid could have wiped out the dinosaurs in just hours or days.

Another idea is that the end came over a long period of time. There is evidence that volcanoes were active around the time the dinosaurs disappeared. If volcanic activity was heavy throughout the world, smoke, ash, and gas could have blocked out the sun and cooled the climate. Much of the food supply for herbivores would have been destroyed. When the herbivores starved, carnivores would have lost their food supply and died, too.

When dinosaurs vanished, many small mammals survived. Scientists believe that because they were so small, they were able to live on very little food. They could have escaped heat by digging into the ground.

After the dinosaurs disappeared, mammals grew larger and larger. Giant forms of early elephants, tigers, bears, and whales lived between 66 million years ago and 10,000 years ago. Some of these huge mammals died out when the Ice Age reduced the amount of food available. Many were hunted by humans. But in many cases, they evolved into smaller animals that are still around today.

Mammoths were one of the biggest mammals. They are relatives of modern elephants. Mammoths had curved tusks and grew 7 to 14 feet tall. They died out around the end of the Ice Age.

Smilodon, the saber-toothed tiger, lived 2.5 million to 10,000 years ago. It hunted large herbivores and is known for its curved front teeth. Modern tigers are distant relatives of *Smilodon*.

As mammals grew bigger a new line of animal closely related to apes evolved around 6 million years ago. Over millions of years, this line evolved. As it evolved, it

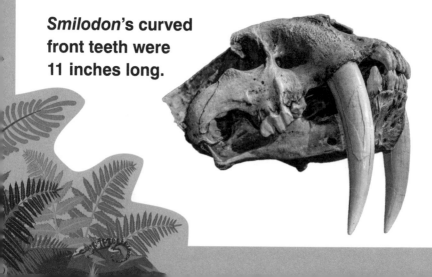

Smilodon's curved front teeth were 11 inches long.

One humanlike species, *Homo habilis*, lived about 1.5 to 2.3 million years ago.

got smarter. It stood up straighter. We would have recognized it as being like us. These new animals had large, well-developed brains. They made tools and communicated. By 200,000 years ago this line evolved into modern humans, the same species as all of us, and by 60,000 years ago had begun spreading around the world.

THE SURVIVORS

Why did some animals survive when the dinosaurs died? When something huge changes in the environment, many animal species cannot survive. The survivors are able to live in conditions that killed off others. It might be because of what survivors eat, where they live, or how they are shaped.

Alligator gars

Tadpole shrimp

When the dinosaurs became extinct, most of the survivors lived in water. Survivors included great white sharks, alligator gars (fish with crocodile-shaped jaws), horseshoe crabs (which have blood that fights bacteria), and lamprey eels (which can attach their mouths to other fish and suck their blood).

Horseshoe crabs

Tuatara

Nautilus

Great white shark

RESOURCES

Many museums and parks have dinosaur fossils on display. Some try to help visitors understand what the world was like in the Age of Dinosaurs. Some let you touch the bones. At a few, you can watch paleontologists at work.

MUSEUMS WITH DINOSAURS

American Museum of Natural History
New York, New York
www.amnh.org

Carnegie Museum of Natural History
Pittsburgh, Pennsylvania
www.carnegiemnh.org

Denver Museum of Nature & Science
Denver, Colorado
www.dmns.org

Dinosaur Discovery Museum
Kenosha, Wisconsin
www.kenosha.org/ wp-dinosaur

Dinosaur National Monument
Dinosaur, Colorado
www.nps.gov/dino

Dinosaur Provincial Park
Brooks, Alberta, Canada
www.albertaparks.ca/ dinosaur.aspx

Dinosaur State Park
Rocky Hill, Connecticut
www.dinosaurstatepark. org

Field Museum of Natural History
Chicago, Illinois
www.fieldmuseum.org

Natural History Museum of Los Angeles County
Los Angeles, California
www.nhm.org

Royal Tyrrell Museum
Drumheller, Alberta,
Canada
www.tyrrellmuseum.com

Science Museum of
Minnesota
St. Paul, Minnesota
www.smm.org

Wyoming
Dinosaur Center
Thermopolis,
Wyoming
www.wyodino.org

Yale Peabody Museum of
Natural History
New Haven, Connecticut
www.peabody.yale.edu

BOOKS

Boy, Were We Wrong About Dinosaurs!, by Kathleen V. Kudlinski (Frances Lincoln Children's Books)

Digging Dinosaurs: The Search That Unraveled the Mystery of Baby Dinosaurs, by John R. Horner and James Gorman (Perennial Library)

Discovery Dinopedia: The Complete Guide to Everything Dinosaur, by the Discovery Channel (Discovery/Time)

WEBSITES TO CHECK OUT

DinoBuzz from University of California Museum of Paleontology
www.ucmp.berkeley.edu/diapsids/dinobuzz.html

Dinosaurs from Discovery Kids
www.discoverykids.com/category/dinosaurs

Zoom Dinosaurs from Enchanted Learning
www.enchantedlearning.com/subjects/dinosaurs

DINOSAUR PRONUNCIATION GUIDE

Allosaurus (al-oh-SORE-us)

Anhanguera (ahn-han-GAIR-ah)

Ankylosaurus (an-ky-loh-SORE-us)

Apatosaurus (uh-PA-toh-sore-us)

Archaeopteryx (ar-kee-OP-tur-iks)

Argentinosaurus (ahr-jen-TEE-noh-sore-us)

Brachiosaurus (BRA-key-oh-sore-us)

Brontosaurus (bron-tuh-SORE-us)

Camarasaurus (KAM-a-rah-sore-us)

Carcharodontosaurus (car-ca-roh-DON-tih-sore-us)

Coelophysis (see-lo-FIE-sis)

Deinonychus (dy-NAH-nih-kus)

Dilophosaurus (die-loh-foe-SORE-us)

Diplodocus (dih-PLAH-duh-kuss)

Drinker (DRIN-kur)

Dryosaurus (DRY-oh-sore-us)

Edmontosaurus (ed-MAHN-toh-sore-us)

Eoraptor (EE-oh-rap-tore)

Gigantoraptor (JY-gant-oh-rap-tore)

Gigantspinosaurus (JY-gant-spy-noh-sore-us)

Hadrosaurus (hay-droh-SORE-us)

Herrerasaurus (huh-rare-uh-SORE-us)

Iguanodon (ih-GWA-noh-don)

Kentrosaurus (KEN-troh-SORE-us)

Maiasaura (my-ya-SORE-a)

Massospondylus (mas-oh-SPON-dih-lus)

Minmi (MIN-mee)

Nodosaurus (NO-doh-sore-us)

Ornithomimus (or-nih-thoh-MY-mus)

Oviraptor (OH-vih-rap-tore)

Pachycephalosaurus (pak-ih-seff-uh-loh-SORE-us)

Parasaurolophus (PAR-ah-sore-ah-loh-fuss)

Polacanthus (pol-uh-KAN-thuss)

Protoceratops (proh-toh-SERR-a-tops)

Psittacosaurus (sit-ah-koh-SORE-us)

Qianzhousaurus (key-an-shoo-SORE-us)

Quetzalcoatlus (kwet-sal-KOH-at-lus)

Spinosaurus (SPY-no-sore-us)

Stegoceras (steh-go-SAIR-us)

Stegosaurus (STEH-go-sore-us)

Styracosaurus (sty-RAK-oh-sore-us)

Tawa (TAH-wah)

Therizinosaurus (theh-rih-ZEE-noh-sore-us

Triceratops (try-SERR-a-tops)

Troodon (TROH-uh-don)

Tyrannosaurus (tie-RAN-oh-sore-us)

Velociraptor (vuh-LAH-si-rap-tore)

Vulcanodon (vull-KAN-uh-don)

Yangchuanosaurus (YANG-shwan-oh-sore-us)

Zhenyuanlong suni (jen-HWAN-long SOO-nee)

Zuniceratops (zoo-nee-SERR-a-tops)

INDEX

Illustrations are indicated by **boldface**. When they fall within a page span, the entire span is **boldface**.

A

Age of dinosaurs **4**, 4–15, 52
Allosaurus 15, 20, **20**, 27, **27**
Anhanguera 53
Ankylosaurus and *ankylosaurs* **10**, 11, 75–76, 80–81, **81**, 83, **83**
Apatosaurus 10, 15, 61–63, **63**
Archaeopteryx 13, **13**, 46, **46**, 48–49
Argentinosaurus 38, **38**, 44, **44–45**, 61

B

Babies and families **38**, 38–45, **43–45**, 58, 61
Birds and feathers 19, 22–24, **24**, 40, **46**, 46–53, **51**, 86
Brachiosaurus 10, **10**, 12, **12**, 54, **54**, 59, 66, **66**
Brontosaurus 62

C

Camarasaurus 59
Carcharodontosaurus 20, 21, **22–23**
Coelophysis 14, 26, **26**

D

Deinonychus 13, **13**, 15, 19, 25, 50
Dilophosaurus 15
Diplodocus 15, 61
Drinker 42
Dryosaurus 15, 88

E

Edmontosaurus 87, 91, **91**
Eggs and nests 7, **38**, 38–41, 43, **43**, 61, 86
Eoraptor 14, 40, 56, **57**
Eras and time periods 14–15, 19, 21, 22, 26, 53, 56, 58–60, 75, 80, 90, 97
Evolution 6, 7, 47, 51–53, 103–107, **104–107**
Extinction 5–6, 15, 101–107

F

Fighting 31, 89, 98–99, **99**
Food and eating 66–73
  carnivores 9, 14, 29–30, **34**, 50, 67–73, **69**, 81, 101, 102
  herbivores 10–11, 15, 56, **66**, 66–68, 70–72, 75, 98, 102, 104
  hunting and foraging 9, 18, 19, 25, 33–35, **34**, 41, 44, **66**, **69**
  omnivores, insectivores and piscivores 56, 67–68, **69**
Fossilized poop (coprolites) 7, 72–73, **72–73**
Fossils and skeletons 6–9, **9**, 26–27, **27**, 36–37, **37**, 43, **43**, 53, 62–65, **63–65**, 86–87, 91, **91**, **97**

G

Gigantoraptor 40
Gigantspinosaurus **78–79**, 79

H

Hadrosaurus and *hadrosaurs* 11, **11**, 86, 89–90, **90**
Herds 44–45, **44–45**, 59, 79
Herrerasaurus 14, 19
Humans 12, **12**, 103, 105, **105**

I

Iguanodon 11, 86, 88–89, **88–89**

K

Kentrosaurus 74, **74**, 79

M

Maiasaura **43**, 86, **90**
Mammals and mammoths 103–105, **105**
Marginocephalians 10, 11, **11**, **92**, 92–97, **94**, **97**, **99**
Massospondylus 15, 56
Minmi 80

N

Nodosaurus 80

O

Orders and types 5–13, **12–13**
Ornithomimus 22
Ornithopods 10–11, **11**, **84**, 84–90, **88–91**
Oviraptor 25, 50

P

Pachycephalosaurus 97, **97**
Parasaurolophus 15, 84, **84**
Polacanthus 80
Protoceratops 98–99, **99**
Psittacosaurus 15, 95
Pterosaurs **46**, 46–53, **48–49**, **51–53**

Q

Qianzhousaurus 32
Quetzalcoatlus **52–53**, 53

S

Sauropods 10, **10**, **54**, 54–63, **57**, **60**, **63**
Smart dinosaurs 19, 35, 50, 98
Spinosaurus 20–21, **20–21**, 69, **69**
Stegoceras 11, 97
Stegosaurus and stegosaurs 10–11, 12, **13**, 15, 75–82, **77**, 78, **82**
Styracosaurus 68, 92, **92**
Survival skills 7, 82–83, **82–83**, 89, 103–107
Survivors of dinosaur age 106–107, **106–107**

T

Tawa 19
Teeth 18–19, 21, **21**, 23, **28**, 29, 30, 33–35, **34**, **65**, 68–70, **69–70**, 87–89, 95, 104, **104**
Therizinosaurus 25
Theropods 9, **16**, 16–27, **20–28**, 29–30, 32, **34**, 47, **51**, 51–53, 98, **99**
Thyreophorans 10–11, **11**, **74**, 74–83, **77–79**, **81–83**
Titanosaurs **60**, 60–61
Triceratops 11, **11**, 15, 33, 68, 93–96, **94**, 101
Troodon 9, **9**, 19
Tyrannosaurus rex (*T-rex*) 9, 15, 16, **16**, 18, 21, 22, **28**, 28–37, **34**, **37**, 42, 64–65, **64–65**, 96, **100**

V

Velociraptor 16, **16**, **24–25**, 25, **48–49**, 50–51, **51**, 98–99, **99**
Vulcanodon 56–57

Y

Yangchuanosaurus 12, **12**

Z

Zhenyuanlong suni 50
Zuniceratops 13, **13**

CREDITS AND ACKNOWLEDGMENTS

Writer Lori Stein

Produced by Scout Books & Media Inc

President and Project Director Susan Knopf

Project Manager Brittany Gialanella

Copyeditor Beth Adelman, Michael Centore

Proofreader Chelsea Burris

Designer Annemarie Redmond

Advisors Michael Rentz, PhD, *Lecturer in Mammology, Iowa State University;* Dr. Joseph Sertich, *Curator of Vertebrate Paleontology, Denver Museum of Nature and Science*

Thanks to the Time Inc. Books team: Margot Schupf, Anja Schmidt, Beth Sutinis, Deirdre Langeland, Georgia Morrissey, Megan Pearlman, Melodie George, and Sue Chodakiewicz.

Special thanks to the Discovery and Animal Planet Creative and Licensing Teams: Denny Chen, Tracy Conner, Elizabeta Ealy, Robert Marick, Doris Miller, Sue Perez-Jackson, and Janet Tsuei.